PRACTICE WORKBOOK
Level 3

Stephen S. Willoughby
Carl Bereiter
Peter Hilton
Joseph H. Rubinstein

SRA
McGraw-Hill

Columbus, Ohio

A Division of The McGraw-Hill Companies

Cover Credits
Photo, Fotosmith; **Design and Illustration,** Morgan-Cain and Associates

SRA/McGraw-Hill
*A Division of The **McGraw·Hill** Companies*

Imprint 2003

Copyright ©1998 by SRA/McGraw-Hill. All rights reserved. Except as permitted under the United States Copyright Act, no part of this publication may be reproduced or distributed in any form or by any means, or stored in a database or retrieval system, without prior written permission from the publisher.

Printed in the United States of America.

Send all inquiries to:
SRA/McGraw-Hill
8787 Orion Place
Columbus, OH 43240-4027

ISBN: 0-02-674243-8

12 13 14 15 POH 05

TABLE OF CONTENTS ◆ PRACTICE

LESSON 1 1	LESSON 43 43
LESSON 2 2	LESSON 44 44
LESSON 3 3	LESSON 45 45
LESSON 4 4	LESSON 46 46
LESSON 5 5	LESSON 47 47
LESSON 6 6	LESSON 48 48
LESSON 7 7	LESSON 49 49
LESSON 8 8	LESSON 50 50
LESSON 9 9	LESSON 51 51
LESSON 10 10	LESSON 52 52
LESSON 11 11	LESSON 53 53
LESSON 12 12	LESSON 54 54
LESSON 13 13	LESSON 55 55
LESSON 14 14	LESSON 56 56
LESSON 15 15	LESSON 57 57
LESSON 16 16	LESSON 58 58
LESSON 17 17	LESSON 59 59
LESSON 18 18	LESSON 60 60
LESSON 19 19	LESSON 61 61
LESSON 20 20	LESSON 62 62
LESSON 21 21	LESSON 63 63
LESSON 22 22	LESSON 64 64
LESSON 23 23	LESSON 65 65
LESSON 24 24	LESSON 66 66
LESSON 25 25	LESSON 67 67
LESSON 26 26	LESSON 68 68
LESSON 27 27	LESSON 69 69
LESSON 28 28	LESSON 70 70
LESSON 29 29	LESSON 71 71
LESSON 30 30	LESSON 72 72
LESSON 31 31	LESSON 73 73
LESSON 32 32	LESSON 74 74
LESSON 33 33	LESSON 75 75
LESSON 34 34	LESSON 76 76
LESSON 35 35	LESSON 77 77
LESSON 36 36	LESSON 78 78
LESSON 37 37	LESSON 79 79
LESSON 38 38	LESSON 80 80
LESSON 39 39	LESSON 81 81
LESSON 40 40	LESSON 82 82
LESSON 41 41	LESSON 83 83
LESSON 42 42	LESSON 84 84

Math Explorations and Applications Level 3

TABLE OF CONTENTS ◆ PRACTICE (Continued)

LESSON 85	85	LESSON 121	121
LESSON 86	86	LESSON 122	122
LESSON 87	87	LESSON 123	123
LESSON 88	88	LESSON 124	124
LESSON 89	89	LESSON 125	125
LESSON 90	90	LESSON 126	126
LESSON 91	91	LESSON 127	127
LESSON 92	92	LESSON 128	128
LESSON 93	93	LESSON 129	129
LESSON 94	94	LESSON 130	130
LESSON 95	95	LESSON 131	131
LESSON 96	96	LESSON 132	132
LESSON 97	97	LESSON 133	133
LESSON 98	98	LESSON 134	134
LESSON 99	99	LESSON 135	135
LESSON 100	100	LESSON 136	136
LESSON 101	101	LESSON 137	137
LESSON 102	102	LESSON 138	138
LESSON 103	103	LESSON 139	139
LESSON 104	104	LESSON 140	140
LESSON 105	105	LESSON 141	141
LESSON 106	106	LESSON 142	142
LESSON 107	107	LESSON 143	143
LESSON 108	108	LESSON 144	144
LESSON 109	109	LESSON 145	145
LESSON 110	110	LESSON 146	146
LESSON 111	111	LESSON 147	147
LESSON 112	112	LESSON 148	148
LESSON 113	113	LESSON 149	149
LESSON 114	114	LESSON 150	150
LESSON 115	115	LESSON 151	151
LESSON 116	116	LESSON 152	152
LESSON 117	117	LESSON 153	153
LESSON 118	118	LESSON 154	154
LESSON 119	119		
LESSON 120	120		

Math Explorations and Applications Level 3

LESSON 1 PRACTICE

Name _____

Find the numbers that are written twice.

① Start counting from 12.

12 14 16 17 11 9 15 12 8 10 17 13 18 _____

② Start counting from 83.

78 85 83 82 80 88 84 83 79 85 81 86 87 _____

③ Start counting from 99.

100 105 102 99 101 98 103 104 109 107 101 103 _____

④ Start counting from 208.

206 210 211 214 208 212 217 214 209 218 207 208 _____

⑤ Start counting from 350.

345 352 350 357 351 353 348 352 349 346 357 347 _____

LESSON 2 PRACTICE

Name _____

Count up. Fill in the missing numbers.

1. | 19 | | | 22 | | | | 26 |

2. | 130 | | | | 134 | | 136 |

3. | 358 | | | | 362 | | 364 |

4. | 706 | | | 709 | | | 712 |

Count down. Fill in the missing numbers.

5. | 33 | 32 | | | | | 27 |

6. | 424 | 423 | | | | | 418 |

7. | 692 | | | | 688 | | 686 |

8. | 1000 | | | | | | 994 |

Count up or down. Fill in the missing numbers.

9. | 699 | | | 696 | | | 693 |

10. | 109 | | | | 113 | | 115 |

2 • Math Explorations and Applications Level 3

LESSON 3 PRACTICE

Name _____

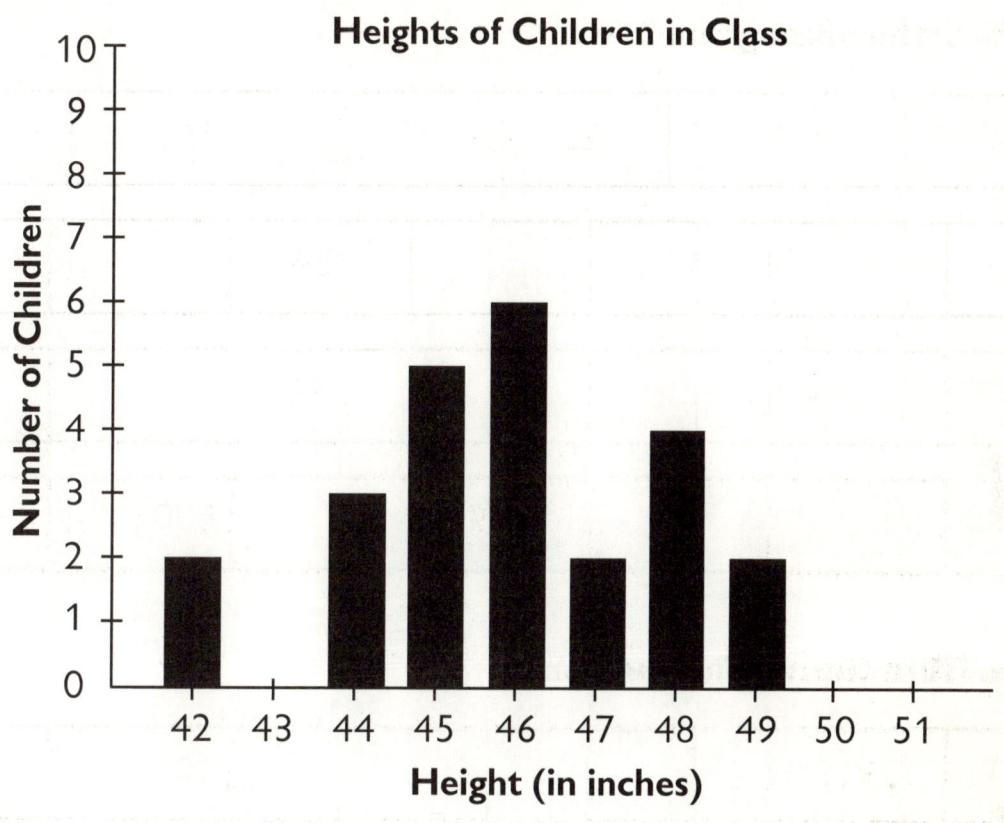

 Use the graph to answer these questions.

1. How many children are 45 inches tall? _____

2. How many more children are 46 inches tall than are 49 inches tall? _____

3. How many children are in the class? _____

4. Which height are most of the children? _____

5. Which heights are the fewest children? _____

6. How many more children are 48 inches tall than are 42 inches tall? _____

LESSON 4 PRACTICE

Name _____

Count up. Fill in the missing numbers.

1.
| 1627 | 1628 | | | 1631 | |

2.
| 3807 | 3808 | | | | 3812 |

3.
| 5009 | 5010 | | | | |

4.
| 7998 | | | | 8002 | |

Count down. Fill in the missing numbers.

5.
| 1012 | 1011 | | | 1008 | |

6.
| 4784 | 4783 | | | | 4779 |

7.
| 6003 | | | 6000 | | 5998 |

8.
| 10,000 | | 9998 | | | |

Count up or down. Fill in the missing numbers.

9.
| 6789 | | | | 6793 | |

10.
| 4321 | | | 4318 | | |

4 • Math Explorations and Applications Level 3

LESSON 5 PRACTICE   Name _____

Tell what place the underlined number is in.

❶ 4<u>6</u>5 _____   ❷ 2<u>1</u>0 _____

❸ <u>1</u>348 _____   ❹ <u>34</u>231 _____

❺ 70<u>3</u> _____   ❻ 943<u>6</u> _____

❼ <u>8</u>5 _____   ❽ <u>7</u>8 _____

❾ 12,<u>7</u>60 _____   ❿ 4<u>1</u>78 _____

Write the least number you can make using each of the digits once.

⓫ 3 and 8 _____   ⓬ 7, 8, and 9 _____

⓭ 5 and 7 _____   ⓮ 4, 3, 2, and 1 _____

⓯ 8, 6, and 5 _____   ⓰ 9, 6, and 3 _____

Write all the three-digit numbers you can make using each of the digits once.

⓱ 2, 3, and 4 _____

⓲ 7, 8, and 9 _____

⓳ 8, 6, and 4 _____

⓴ Make a two-digit number in which both digits are the same and the sum of the digits is 8. _____

㉑ Make a three-digit number in which all three digits are the same and the sum of the digits is 9. _____

㉒ Make a four-digit number in which all four digits are the same and the sum of the digits is 16. _____

LESSON 6 PRACTICE

Name _____

Add.

① 6 + 6 = _____   ② 10 + 5 = _____   ③ 7 + 7 = _____

④ 9 + 7 = _____   ⑤ 5 + 6 = _____   ⑥ 3 + 5 = _____

⑦   10   ⑧   9   ⑨   7
   + 8   + 9   + 3

⑩   5   ⑪   5   ⑫   10
   + 4   + 5   + 6

Subtract.

⑬ 15 − 6 = _____   ⑭ 12 − 5 = _____   ⑮ 17 − 9 = _____

⑯ 10 − 7 = _____   ⑰ 8 − 4 = _____   ⑱ 20 − 10 = _____

⑲   11   ⑳   9   ㉑   13
   − 8   − 3   − 6

㉒   10   ㉓   16   ㉔   14
   − 4   − 6   − 7

LESSON 7 PRACTICE Name _____

Solve. Watch the signs.

1. $5 + \boxed{} = 14$

2. $\boxed{} + 9 = 14$

3. $7 + \boxed{} = 16$

4. $\boxed{} + 4 = 12$

5. $13 - \boxed{} = 7$

6. $\boxed{} - 8 = 8$

7. $\boxed{} + 3 = 12$

8. $6 + \boxed{} = 13$

9. $\boxed{} - 6 = 10$

10. $12 - \boxed{} = 7$

11. $20 - \boxed{} = 15$

12. $\boxed{} - 3 = 8$

13. $8 + \boxed{} = 13$

14. $\boxed{} - 2 = 8$

15. $\boxed{} - 3 = 9$

16. $2 + \boxed{} = 12$

17. $\boxed{} + 6 = 11$

18. $\boxed{} - 7 = 7$

19. $11 - \boxed{} = 5$

20. $\boxed{} - 5 = 0$

Math Explorations and Applications Level 3 • 7

LESSON 8 PRACTICE

Name _____

Solve. Watch the signs.

① 3 + 7	② 8 − 1	③ 9 + 6	④ 7 + 5	⑤ 13 − 4
⑥ 4 − 2	⑦ 5 + 5	⑧ 11 − 6	⑨ 10 − 9	⑩ 8 + 7
⑪ 9 + 3	⑫ 18 − 9	⑬ 6 + 6	⑭ 4 + 8	⑮ 14 − 5

⑯ 7 + 7 = _____ ⑰ 12 − 4 = _____ ⑱ 17 − 9 = _____

⑲ 4 − 1 = _____ ⑳ 1 + 9 = _____ ㉑ 10 + 6 = _____

㉒ 13 − 7 = _____ ㉓ 2 + 3 = _____ ㉔ 7 − 2 = _____

㉕ 8 + 0 = _____ ㉖ 13 − 5 = _____ ㉗ 15 − 6 = _____

㉘ 5 + 6 = _____ ㉙ 3 − 3 = _____ ㉚ 5 + 8 = _____

8 • Math Explorations and Applications Level 3

LESSON 9 PRACTICE

Name _____

Solve these problems.

❶ Tracy has five cookies, and Mario has three cookies. How many more cookies does Tracy have? _____

❷ Tracy's brother bakes 12 more cookies. He gives eight more cookies to Tracy to share with her friend. How many cookies does Tracy have now? _____

❸ Of the 12 cookies Tracy's brother baked, how many cookies are left after he gives eight of them to Tracy? _____

❹ Don has $13. He buys a new ball. Don has $8 left. How much did he spend? _____

❺ Don walks the neighbor's dog and earns $4. How much does he have now? _____

❻ How many more dollars must Don earn to have $17? _____

Math Explorations and Applications Level 3 • 9

LESSON 10 PRACTICE

Name _____

Solve. Watch the signs.

① 5 + 5 − 3 = _____

② 6 + 8 − 4 = _____

③ 6 − 4 + 7 = _____

④ 11 − 5 + 8 = _____

⑤ 14 − 5 + 2 = _____

⑥ 12 − 9 + 3 = _____

⑦ 9 + 3 − 1 + 4 = _____

⑧ 7 + 2 − 8 + 6 = _____

⑨ 13 − 5 + 2 − 3 = _____

⑩ 16 − 6 + 4 − 3 = _____

⑪ 4 + 4 + 4 − 6 + 3 = _____

⑫ 9 + 6 − 7 − 2 + 4 = _____

⑬ 2 + 2 + 2 + 2 + 2 − 8 = _____

⑭ 8 − 7 + 3 + 3 + 3 + 3 = _____

⑮ 16 − 3 − 8 + 4 − 6 + 7 + 9 = _____

⑯ 4 + 3 + 12 − 8 + 5 − 7 = _____

LESSON 11 PRACTICE

Name _____

Tell whether each number is odd or even.

1. 403 _____
2. 60 _____
3. 718 _____
4. 24 _____
5. 111 _____
6. 32 _____
7. 19 _____
8. 713 _____

Ring the incorrect answers.

9. 26 + 16 = 42
10. 57 + 11 = 69
11. 43 + 10 = 53
12. 14 + 28 = 43
13. 38 + 12 = 50
14. 24 + 17 = 40
15. 49 + 22 = 71
16. 13 + 15 = 28
17. 44 + 14 = 57
18. 27 + 36 = 62
19. 17 + 47 = 64
20. 72 + 14 = 86

Write *odd* or *even* in each blank below.

21. If you add two even numbers, the sum is an _____ number.

22. If you add two odd numbers, the sum is an _____ number.

23. If you add an even number and an odd number, the sum is an _____ number.

LESSON 12 PRACTICE

Name _____

Check your math skills.

❶ 5 + 6 = _____

❷ 3 + 6 = _____

❸ 8 + 9 = _____

❹ 20 – 10 = _____

❺ 14 – 4 = _____

❻ 15 – 7 = _____

❼ 7 + 4 = _____

❽ 10 + 6 = _____

❾ 12 – 4 = _____

❿ 16 – 7 = _____

⓫ 17 – 8 = _____

⓬ 6 + 9 = _____

⓭ 4 + 8 = _____

⓮ 8 + 6 = _____

⓯ 13 – 6 = _____

⓰ 14 – 7 = _____

⓱ 11 – 3 = _____

⓲ 2 + 9 = _____

⓳ 7 + 1 = _____

⓴ 18 – 9 = _____

Number correct last time ☐

Number correct this time ☐

Difference ☐

12 • Math Explorations and Applications Level 3

LESSON 13 PRACTICE   Name _____

Write the standard number for each of these.

1. 3 tens and 4 = _____
2. 6 tens and 0 = _____
3. 3 tens and 14 = _____
4. 7 tens and 0 = _____
5. 5 tens and 14 = _____
6. 7 tens and 10 = _____
7. 5 tens and 17 = _____
8. 7 tens and 18 = _____
9. 0 tens and 17 = _____
10. 15 tens = _____
11. 1 ten and 12 = _____
12. 16 tens = _____
13. 17 tens = _____
14. 18 tens = _____
15. 17 hundreds = _____
16. 12 hundreds = _____
17. 3 hundreds and 7 tens = _____
18. 4 hundreds and 10 tens = _____
19. 3 hundreds and 17 tens = _____
20. 1 hundred and 7 tens = _____
21. 1 hundred and 13 tens = _____
22. 7 hundreds and 12 tens = _____
23. 6 hundreds and 11 tens = _____
24. 6 hundreds and 1 ten = _____

Math Explorations and Applications Level 3 • 13

LESSON 14 PRACTICE

Name _____

Add.

1) 45
   + 16

2) 58
   + 25

3) 74
   + 8

4) 36
   + 46

5) 29
   + 14

6) 17
   + 43

7) 56
   + 18

8) 47
   + 24

9) 13
   + 18

10) 55
   + 23

11) 42
   + 18

12) 37
   + 28

13) 29
   + 32

14) 27
   + 16

15) 14
   + 59

16) 75
   + 20

17) 33
   + 49

18) 21
   + 69

19) 76
   + 15

20) 49
   + 39

14 • Math Explorations and Applications Level 3

LESSON 15 PRACTICE

Name _____

Rewrite to show ten more ones.

1. 34 = _____ tens and _____
2. 38 = _____ tens and _____
3. 40 = _____ tens and _____
4. 50 = _____ tens and _____
5. 57 = _____ tens and _____

Rewrite to show ten more tens.

6. 240 = _____ hundreds and _____ tens
7. 290 = _____ hundreds and _____ tens
8. 300 = _____ hundreds and _____ tens
9. 330 = _____ hundreds and _____ tens
10. 420 = _____ hundreds and _____ tens

First write the number. Then rewrite it to show ten more ones.

11. 402 = _____ hundreds, _____ tens, and _____ =
    _____ hundreds, _____ tens, and _____

12. 508 = _____ hundreds, _____ tens, and _____ =
    _____ hundreds, _____ tens, and _____

Math Explorations and Applications Level 3

LESSON 16 PRACTICE

Name _____

Subtract.

1) 75
  − 28

2) 63
  − 14

3) 91
  − 28

4) 84
  − 36

5) 32
  − 15

6) 40
  − 28

7) 58
  − 19

8) 29
  − 19

9) 46
  − 19

10) 60
  − 34

11) 82
  − 71

12) 26
  − 18

13) 97
  − 59

14) 19
  − 14

15) 43
  − 25

16) 68
  − 49

17) 51
  − 23

18) 94
  − 50

19) 65
  − 27

20) 44
  − 27

LESSON 17 PRACTICE

Name _____

Solve these problems.

① There are 29 children in Mrs. Moore's class. Twelve are girls. How many boys are in Mrs. Moore's class? _____

② There are two third-grade classes. In one class there are 27 students. In the other class there are 29 students. How many students are there all together in the two classes? _____

③ Nancy has 63¢, and Vera has 29¢. How much money do they have all together? _____

④ How much more money does Nancy have? _____

Ruben rode his bike 15 blocks east from his home. He then turned around and rode nine blocks west.

⑤ How many blocks is Ruben from home? _____

⑥ How many blocks did Ruben ride all together? _____

Math Explorations and Applications Level 3 • 17

LESSON 18 PRACTICE

Name _____

 Solve these problems.

① How much would the doll and the rubber ball cost? _____

② How much would the crayons, the top, and the rubber ball cost? _____

③ How much would the top and the bracelet cost? _____

④ How much would the top, the candy bar, and the crayons cost? _____

⑤ Lauren has $1. Without buying more than one of the same item, what is the greatest number of items Lauren can buy? _____

⑥ What pairs of items can Lauren buy for $1?

_____

LESSON 19 PRACTICE

Name _____

Solve. Watch the signs.

1. 25
   + 57

2. 43
   + 18

3. 66
   − 27

4. 14
   + 56

5. 48
   − 17

6. 42
   + 27

7. 62
   − 36

8. 35
   + 48

9. 19
   + 26

10. 84
    − 65

11. 93
    − 27

12. 31
    + 49

13. 32
    − 17

14. 76
    − 29

15. 27
    + 38

16. 80
    − 42

17. 60
    + 12

18. 95
    − 26

19. 42
    − 17

20. 54
    + 28

LESSON 20 PRACTICE

Name _____

Solve. Watch the signs.

1) 34
   − 17

2) 29
   + 23

3) 70
   − 25

4) 13
   + 45

5) 51
   − 36

6) 97
   − 14

7) 53
   + 37

8) 16
   + 26

9) 66
   − 8

10) 40
   − 38

11) 19
   + 7

12) 78
   − 58

13) 93
   − 34

14) 39
   + 15

15) 38
   + 28

16) 48
   − 26

17) 85
   − 72

18) 41
   − 37

19) 38
   + 49

20) 17
   + 57

Number correct last time ☐

Number correct this time ☐

Difference ☐

LESSON 21 PRACTICE

Name _____

Solve. Watch the signs.

1. 416 + 204

2. 307 − 128

3. 475 + 125

4. 537 + 358

5. 602 − 487

6. 735 + 145

7. 405 − 288

8. 125 + 125

9. 700 − 298

10. 350 + 270

11. 900 − 600

12. 808 − 639

13. 304 − 167

14. 602 − 415

15. 748 + 175

16. 243 + 689

17. 377 + 298

18. 405 − 345

19. 600 + 300

20. 184 + 609

Math Explorations and Applications Level 3 • **21**

LESSON 22 PRACTICE

Name _____

Solve. Watch the signs.

①   329
    + 136

②   506
    − 237

③   800
    − 275

④   604
    − 359

⑤   233
    + 529

⑥   307
    − 217

⑦   608
    + 248

⑧   901
    − 687

⑨   546
    + 267

⑩   503
    − 144

⑪   405
    + 396

⑫   298
    + 573

⑬   326
    + 474

⑭   426
    + 179

⑮   805
    − 209

⑯   507
    − 398

⑰   600
    − 255

⑱   172
    + 719

⑲   402
    − 397

⑳   200
    − 101

LESSON 23 PRACTICE

Name _____

Solve. Watch the signs.

① 685
  − 276

② 908
  + 437

③ 479
  + 365

④ 504
  − 327

 **Solve these problems.**

Here is the number of baseball cards that each student has.

Leon: 324   Paula: 256   Scott: 437   Robyn: 480

⑤ How many baseball cards do the students have all together? _____

⑥ Who has the most cards? _____

⑦ How many more cards does Leon have than Paula? _____

⑧ How many more cards does Robyn have than Scott? _____

⑨ Does Scott have at least one card from every baseball team? _____

⑩ If Scott gives 24 cards to Paula, how many cards does she have all together? _____

Number correct last time ☐
Number correct this time ☐
Difference ☐

LESSON 24 PRACTICE

Name _____

Solve. Watch the signs.

① 236   ② 350   ③ 784   ④ 237
 + 145   − 162   − 439   + 356

⑤ 306   ⑥ 185   ⑦ 800   ⑧ 347
 − 87   + 245   − 346   − 286

⑨ 107   ⑩ 387   ⑪ 230   ⑫ 820
 − 23   + 136   − 169   − 452

⑬ 64   ⑭ 53   ⑮ 28   ⑯ 37
    22   29   14   12
 + 87   + 24   71   43
                    + 34   + 86

⑰ 73   ⑱ 55   ⑲ 414   ⑳ 48
    76   14   − 173   32
 + 20   28   + 76
          + 85

24 • Math Explorations and Applications Level 3

LESSON 25 PRACTICE   Name _____

Add.

1)
```
   9
   4
+  6
```

2)
```
   8
   7
+  5
```

3)
```
  32
  19
+ 25
```

4)
```
  40
  27
+ 16
```

5)
```
  25
  13
  27
+ 29
```

6)
```
  13
  28
  14
+ 53
```

7)
```
  20
  46
  14
+ 17
```

8)
```
  25
  10
  37
+ 18
```

9)
```
  305
  125
+ 275
```

10)
```
  250
  250
+ 500
```

11)
```
  222
  173
  156
+ 224
```

12)
```
  189
  262
  150
+ 301
```

13)
```
  23
  18
  40
+ 21
```

14)
```
  229
  532
+ 161
```

15)
```
  204
  704
+ 553
```

16)
```
  213
  268
  147
+ 244
```

Number correct last time ☐
Number correct this time ☐
Difference ☐

Math Explorations and Applications Level 3 • 25

LESSON 26 PRACTICE

Name _____

Solve. Watch the signs.

❶ 4136
  + 2545

❷ 3126
  − 1462

❸ 6000
  − 4210

❹ 1855
  + 278

❺ 1328
  − 987

❻ 1235
  + 4647

❼ 2901
  − 1364

❽ 4000
  − 2816

❾   604
    220
  + 837

❿   539
    294
  + 137

⓫   603
    147
    371
  + 294

⓬   375
    129
    536
  + 86

⓭ 7753
  − 4191

⓮   457
     99
  + 108

⓯ 3201
  − 1674

⓰ 1124
  + 6563

⓱ 5354
  − 2263

⓲ 1692
  + 5966

⓳ 3604
  + 597

⓴ 7291
  − 6414

LESSON 27 PRACTICE

Name _____

Solve. Watch the signs.

① 6281   ② 4325   ③ 4000   ④ 2679
  + 1549   − 2572   − 1249   + 348

⑤ 2438   ⑥ 2473   ⑦ 6175   ⑧ 6000
  − 1569   + 2887   − 3746   + 3816

⑨ 4183   ⑩ 7235   ⑪ 2906   ⑫ 3008
  + 1350   − 5827   + 1369   − 1898

⑬ 7946   ⑭ 3887   ⑮ 6579   ⑯ 9365
  + 1164   − 3657   − 2463   − 3868

⑰ 8903   ⑱ 4183   ⑲ 3752   ⑳ 9352
  − 5639   + 1909   − 2837   − 5633

LESSON 28 PRACTICE

Name _____

Solve these problems.

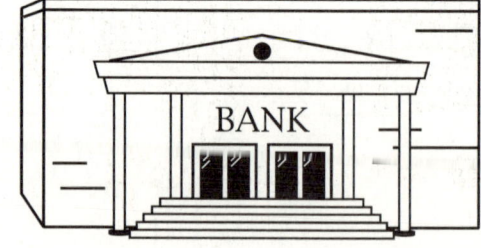

Bonita has $4135 in her college savings account.
Mary has $3298 in her account.

1. Who has more money in her account? _____

2. How much more? _____

3. How much do Bonita and Mary have all together? _____

Sam and Larry collect bottle caps. Sam has 2316 bottle caps, and Larry has 1568.

4. How many more bottle caps does Sam have? _____

5. How many bottle caps do Sam and Larry have all together? _____

6. The telephone was invented in 1876. How many years ago was the telephone invented? _____

7. Reiko planted a garden in the shape of a triangle. The dimensions are 300 meters, 268 meters, and 179 meters. How many meters of fencing would Reiko need to keep the rabbits out of her garden? _____

28 • Math Explorations and Applications Level 3

LESSON 29 PRACTICE

Name _____

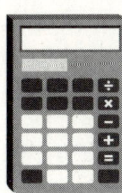 Solve these problems with your calculator and without your calculator. Do you get the same answer each way?

① 6 + 9 = _____

② 12 − 8 = _____

③ 60 + 90 = _____

④ 120 − 80 = _____

⑤ 600 + 900 = _____

⑥ 1200 − 800 = _____

⑦ 6000 + 9000 = _____

⑧ 12,000 − 8,000 = _____

⑨ 7 + 5 + 5 = _____

⑩ 7 + 5 + 5 + 5 + 5 = _____

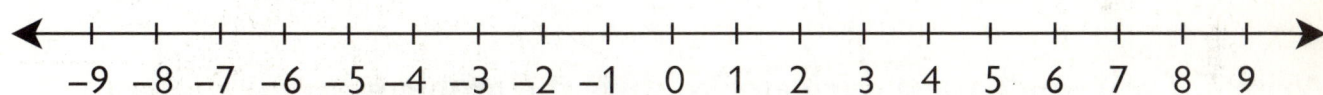

Use the number line to help solve these problems. Also solve them with a calculator. Are the answers the same?

⑪ 9 − 2 − 2 − 2 = _____

⑫ −5 + 3 = _____

⑬ 9 − 2 − 2 − 2 − 2 = _____

⑭ −5 + 3 + 3 = _____

⑮ 8 − 3 − 3 − 3 = _____

⑯ −8 + 4 = _____

⑰ 8 − 3 − 3 − 3 − 3 = _____

⑱ 4 − 7 = _____

⑲ −6 + 9 = _____

⑳ 6 − 9 = _____

Math Explorations and Applications Level 3 • 29

LESSON 30 PRACTICE

Name _____

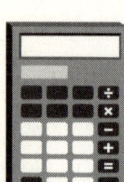 Solve. If you use a calculator, you must push the keys for all the numbers and signs shown.

❶ 3 + 3 = _____   ❷ 7 + 9 = _____

❸ 30 + 30 = _____   ❹ 70 + 90 = _____

❺ 300 + 300 = _____   ❻ 700 + 900 = _____

❼ 14 − 8 = _____   ❽ 140 − 80 = _____

❾ 1400 − 800 = _____   ❿ 10 − 2 = _____

⓫ 100 − 2 = _____   ⓬ 1000 − 2 = _____

Write **C** if you would use a calculator to solve the problem.
Write **N** if you would not. Then solve each problem.

⓭ ◯ 6789 − 5533 = _____   ⓮ ◯ 400 + 600 = _____

⓯ ◯ 1786 − 1777 = _____   ⓰ ◯ 40 + 60 = _____

⓱ ◯ 662 + 338 = _____   ⓲ ◯ 5604 − 2376 = _____

⓳ ◯ 4000 − 2000 = _____   ⓴ ◯ 20 + 20 = _____

㉑ ◯ 8653 + 785 = _____   ㉒ ◯ 900 − 5 = _____

㉓ ◯ 50 + 450 = _____   ㉔ ◯ 6783 − 1998 = _____

LESSON 31 PRACTICE

Name _____

What is the right sign? Draw <, >, or =.

① 15 ◯ 52

② 10,000 ◯ 1000

③ 73 ◯ 39

④ 9540 ◯ 9504

⑤ 112 ◯ 121

⑥ 3206 ◯ 3620

⑦ 237 ◯ 732

⑧ 1400 ◯ 4100

⑨ 560 ◯ 506

⑩ 7283 ◯ 6995

⑪ 320 ◯ 3020

⑫ 5250 ◯ 2550

⑬ 1000 ◯ 989

⑭ 1019 ◯ 119

⑮ 4632 ◯ 4632

⑯ 2168 ◯ 2648

⑰ 1616 ◯ 1661

⑱ 9743 ◯ 7998

⑲ 7800 ◯ 7080

⑳ 7351 ◯ 7315

LESSON 32 PRACTICE

Name _____

Round these numbers to the nearest ten.

① 34 _____   ② 28 _____   ③ 87 _____   ④ 23 _____
⑤ 56 _____   ⑥ 12 _____   ⑦ 41 _____   ⑧ 79 _____

Round these numbers to the nearest hundred.

⑨ 134 _____   ⑩ 899 _____   ⑪ 321 _____   ⑫ 451 _____
⑬ 647 _____   ⑭ 289 _____   ⑮ 709 _____   ⑯ 935 _____

Round these numbers to the nearest thousand.

⑰ 4323 _____   ⑱ 5220 _____   ⑲ 8345 _____   ⑳ 6677 _____
㉑ 7880 _____   ㉒ 1654 _____   ㉓ 9120 _____   ㉔ 3654 _____

Solve these problems.

㉕ Mrs. Worth wants to buy a blouse that costs $38 and a skirt that costs $55. She has $100. Does she have enough money to buy the blouse and skirt? _____

㉖ Mr. Worth wants to buy new appliances. A refrigerator costs $789, and a microwave oven costs $329. He has $1000. Does he have enough money to buy the new appliances? _____

LESSON 33 PRACTICE

Name _____

Choose the correct answer, either by approximating or by using your knowledge of odds and evens.

1. 3948 + 1994 = _____   a. 542   b. 5420   c. 5942
2. 3948 − 1994 = _____   a. 1954   b. 1951   c. 953
3. 7738 + 2008 = _____   a. 8356   b. 9745   c. 9746
4. 7738 − 2008 = _____   a. 5736   b. 5730   c. 506
5. 4862 + 3175 = _____   a. 7038   b. 8037   c. 6038
6. 4862 − 3175 = _____   a. 1687   b. 800   c. 937
7. 1234 + 2468 = _____   a. 702   b. 370   c. 3702
8. 5689 + 82 = _____   a. 5771   b. 5607   c. 1601
9. 2999 − 89 = _____   a. 2910   b. 3028   c. 2820
10. 6220 − 208 = _____   a. 6015   b. 6012   c. 6001

For each of the following problems, give an approximate answer that is within 50 of the correct answer.

11. During four years of playing college basketball, Michael scored a total of 1209 points. Sergio scored a total of 1583 points. About how many more points did Sergio score than Michael?

    _____

12. The scientist Isaac Newton was born in 1642. Albert Einstein was born in 1879. About how many years earlier was Newton born?

    _____

Math Explorations and Applications Level 3 • 33

LESSON 34 PRACTICE

Name _____

What is the right sign? Draw <, >, or =. Use shortcuts when possible.

1. 300 + 50 ◯ 300 + 500
2. 1036 + 5872 ◯ 1035 + 5871
3. 7980 + 980 ◯ 7980 − 80
4. 6380 − 380 ◯ 7000 − 1000
5. 239 + 405 ◯ 40 + 239
6. 543 + 69 ◯ 75 + 67
7. 175 − 100 ◯ 175 − 75
8. 2040 + 653 ◯ 240 + 653
9. 8117 + 53 ◯ 8117 + 62
10. 4000 − 20 ◯ 4000 − 200
11. 500 − 250 ◯ 500 − 450
12. 5980 + 472 ◯ 586 + 5980
13. 6023 + 189 ◯ 189 + 6023
14. 7000 − 500 ◯ 7000 − 5000
15. 275 + 1000 ◯ 275 + 100
16. 980 − 80 ◯ 980 − 900
17. 420 − 67 ◯ 320 − 67
18. 7520 + 5 ◯ 7000 + 525
19. 800 − 428 ◯ 800 − 528
20. 962 − 47 ◯ 962 − 59

LESSON 35 PRACTICE

Name _____

Solve. Watch the signs.

① 13 − 6 = _____ ② 7 + 9 = _____ ③ 16 − 8 = _____

④ 20 − 10 = _____ ⑤ 8 + 4 = _____ ⑥ 6 + 6 = _____

⑦   74
  + 87

⑧ 357
 + 124

⑨   82
 − 34

⑩ 455
 − 239

⑪   64
   33
 + 81

⑫   50
   29
 + 44

⑬   38
   24
   75
 + 14

⑭   30
   13
   54
 + 46

Solve these problems.

⑮ A piece of plywood is in the shape of a triangle. The dimensions are 12 yards, 16 yards, and 15 yards. Find the perimeter. _____

⑯ A piece of carpet is in the shape of a rectangle. The dimensions are 10 feet long and 8 feet wide. Find the perimeter. _____

LESSON 36 PRACTICE

Name _____

In each problem two of the answers are clearly wrong and one is correct. Choose the correct answer.

1 75 + 150 =
- a. 145
- b. 75
- c. 225

2 850 − 164 =
- a. 686
- b. 976
- c. 26

3 507 + 368 =
- a. 425
- b. 875
- c. 8015

4 1179 − 536 =
- a. 1273
- b. 643
- c. 1173

5 4327 + 2581 =
- a. 6908
- b. 378
- c. 3488

6 9085 − 7281 =
- a. 374
- b. 8764
- c. 1804

7 1276 + 2724 =
- a. 6000
- b. 2000
- c. 4000

8 732 − 458 =
- a. 64
- b. 274
- c. 1084

9 9658 + 324 =
- a. 6752
- b. 9982
- c. 2582

10 5468 − 379 =
- a. 2379
- b. 5089
- c. 1589

LESSON 37 PRACTICE

Name _____

What time is it?
How many minutes after the hour?

①
6:15

_____ minutes after _____

②
11:33

_____ minutes after _____

③
1:48

_____ minutes after _____

④
3:05

_____ minutes after _____

How many minutes before the hour?

⑤
4:37

_____ minutes to _____

⑥
9:45

_____ minutes to _____

Math Explorations and Applications Level 3 • **37**

LESSON 38 PRACTICE

Name _____

Tell the time in three ways.

1.  ____:____, _____ minutes after _____, _____ minutes to _____

2.  ____:____, _____ minutes after _____, _____ minutes to _____

3.  ____:____, _____ minutes after _____, _____ minutes to _____

4.  ____:____, _____ minutes after _____, _____ minutes to _____

5.  ____:____, _____ minutes after _____, _____ minutes to _____

6.  ____:____, _____ minutes after _____, _____ minutes to _____

LESSON 39 PRACTICE

Name _____

Solve. Watch the signs.

1. _____ − 6 = 8
2. _____ + 9 = 17
3. 16 − _____ = 7
4. _____ − 10 = 4
5. 8 + _____ = 12
6. 15 − _____ = 9

What is the right sign? Draw <, >, or =.

7. 64 + 22 ◯ 15 + 57
8. 120 + 45 ◯ 150 + 35
9. 38 + 45 ◯ 52 + 31
10. 50 + 38 ◯ 48 + 41

Add.

11. 14
     36
   + 81

12. 20
     49
   + 48

13. 238
     244
     175
   + 14

14. 330
     173
     504
   + 461

Solve these problems.

15. A piece of glass is in the shape of a triangle. The dimensions are 19 inches, 8 inches, and 7 inches. Find the perimeter. _____

16. A piece of fabric is in the shape of a rectangle. The dimensions are 14 feet long and 6 feet wide. Find the perimeter. _____

LESSON 40 PRACTICE

Name _____

Use this code chart to solve the riddle.

A	B	C	D	E	F	G	H	I	J	K	L	M
1	2	3	4	5	6	7	8	9	10	11	12	13

N	O	P	Q	R	S	T	U	V	W	X	Y	Z
14	15	16	17	18	19	20	21	22	23	24	25	26

Riddle:

___ ___ ___ ___
16 + 7   432 − 424   769 − 768   360 − 340

___ ___ ___   ___ ___ ___
20 − 12   90 − 89   12 + 7   88 − 69   4 + 5   15 + 9

___ ___ ___ ___
8 + 4   344 − 339   216 − 209   10 + 9

___ ___ ___
10 − 9   8 + 6   32 − 28

___ ___ ___ ___ ___ ?
24 − 5   21 − 12   7 + 7   35 − 28   11 + 8

Answer: a trio

40 • *Math Explorations and Applications* Level 3

LESSON 41 PRACTICE

Name _____

Solve these problems.

Mrs. Chung is planting a garden.

❶ In which garden would she be able to plant more vegetables? _____

❷ Which garden is shorter? _____

❸ Which garden has a larger area? _____

Tina is cutting out three circles to make a snowman.

❹ Which circle will take the longest to cut out? _____

❺ Which circle has the largest area? _____

❻ Which circle has the smallest area? _____

Ms. Smith drives from home to work and then back home. She drives 4 kilometers north, 2 kilometers east, 4 kilometers south, and then 2 kilometers west.

❼ Draw an outline of the route Ms. Smith takes. _____

Mr. Banks drives from home to work and then back home. He drives 3 kilometers north, 5 kilometers east, 3 kilometers south, and then 5 kilometers west.

❽ Draw an outline of the route Mr. Banks takes. _____

❾ Who drives farther from home to work and then home again, Ms. Smith or Mr. Banks? _____

❿ Which outline surrounds a larger area, Ms. Smith's or Mr. Banks's? _____

Math Explorations and Applications Level 3

LESSON 42 PRACTICE

Name _____

Tell the shaded area of each grid.   1 cm □ 1 square centimeter   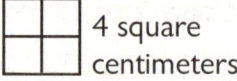 4 square centimeters

❶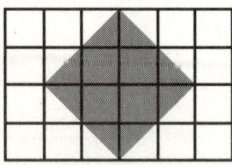

☐ square centimeters

❷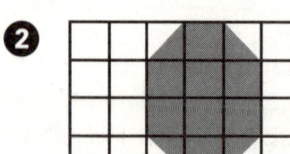

☐ square centimeters

❸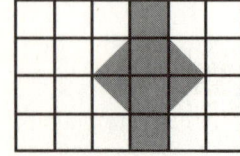

☐ square centimeters

❹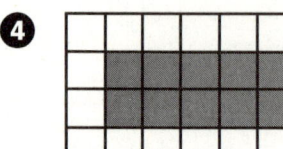

☐ square centimeters

❺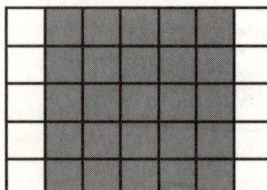

☐ square centimeters

❻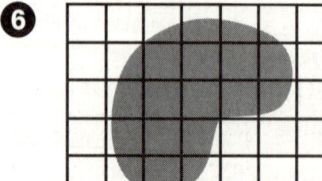

☐ square centimeters

❼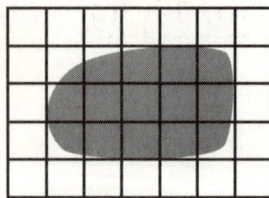

☐ square centimeters

❽

☐ square centimeters

42 • *Math Explorations and Applications* Level 3

LESSON 43 PRACTICE

Name _____

Make three copies of each grid below. Then do each of the following exercises on two grids.

① Color the boxes you reach when counting by 2s. Ring the number in the boxes you reach when counting by 7s. Place an X in the boxes you reach when counting by 6s.

② Ring the number in the boxes you reach when counting by 3s. Place an X in the boxes you reach when counting by 10s.

③ Ring the number in the boxes you reach when counting by 4s. Place an X in the boxes you reach when counting by 8s.

0	1	2	3	4	5	6	7	8	9
10	11	12	13	14	15	16	17	18	19
20	21	22	23	24	25	26	27	28	29
30	31	32	33	34	35	36	37	38	39
40	41	42	43	44	45	46	47	48	49
50	51	52	53	54	55	56	57	58	59
60	61	62	63	64	65	66	67	68	69
70	71	72	73	74	75	76	77	78	79
80	81	82	83	84	85	86	87	88	89
90	91	92	93	94	95	96	97	98	99

0	1	2	3	4	5	6
7	8	9	10	11	12	13
14	15	16	17	18	19	20
21	22	23	24	25	26	27
28	29	30	31	32	33	34
35	36	37	38	39	40	41
42	43	44	45	46	47	48

LESSON 44 PRACTICE

Name _____

Solve these problems.

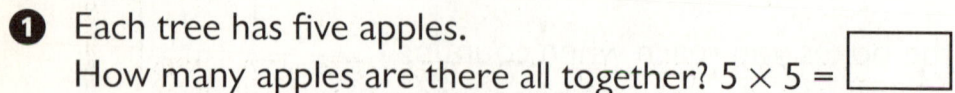

① Each tree has five apples.
How many apples are there all together? 5 × 5 = ☐

② Each carton has six eggs.
How many eggs are there all together? 4 × 6 = ☐

③ Each fishbowl has four fish.
How many fish are there all together? 3 × 4 = ☐

④ Each box has eight pieces of chalk.
How many pieces of chalk are there all together? 2 × 8 = ☐

⑤ Each kite has four sections.
How many sections are there all together? 5 × 4 = ☐

LESSON 45 PRACTICE

Name _____

Many buses have four seats in each row.

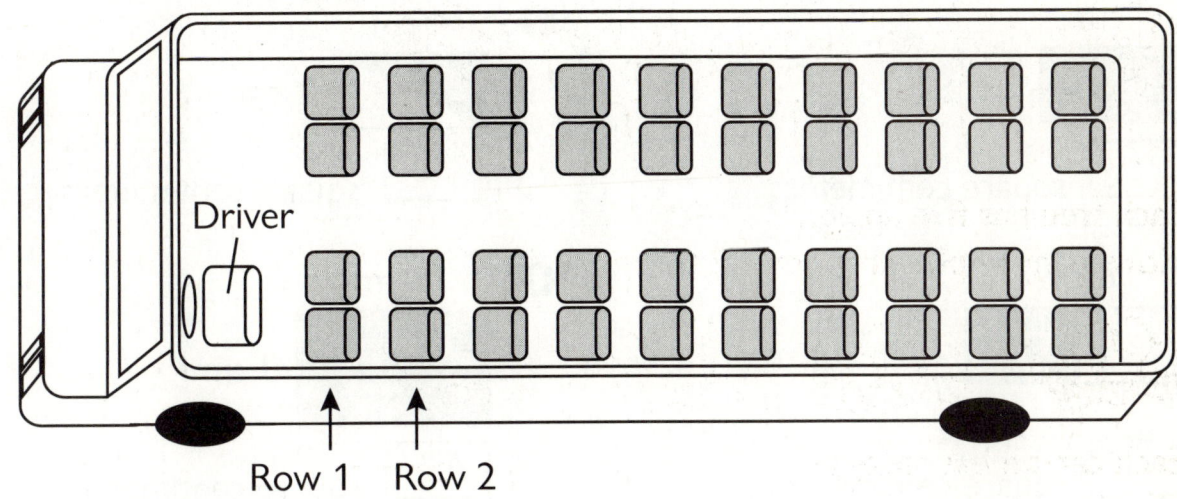

Row 1   Row 2

Answer the following questions about the bus pictured above.

1. How many seats are in the first row? _____

2. How many seats are in the first two rows? _____

3. How many seats are there in the first three rows? _____

4. How many seats are in the first four rows? _____

5. How many seats are in the first five rows? _____

6. How many seats are in the first six rows? _____

7. How many seats are there in the first seven rows? _____

8. How many seats are in the first eight rows? _____

9. How many seats are there in the first nine rows? _____

10. How many seats are in the whole bus? Do not count the driver's seat. _____

Math Explorations and Applications Level 3 • 45

LESSON 46 PRACTICE

Name _____

Estimate the area of the shaded part of each rectangle.

1   4 cm

2 cm

☐ square centimeters

2   4 cm

2 cm

☐ square centimeters

3   6 cm

2 cm

☐ square centimeters

4   5 cm

3 cm

☐ square centimeters

5   4 cm
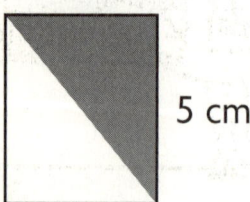
5 cm

☐ square centimeters

6   6 cm
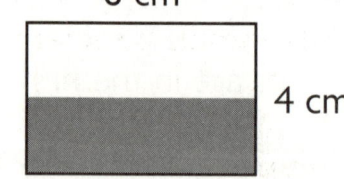
4 cm

☐ square centimeters

7   5 cm
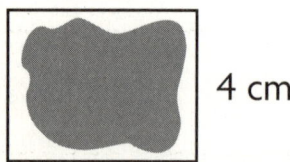
4 cm

☐ square centimeters

8   8 cm

3 cm

☐ square centimeters

9   7 cm
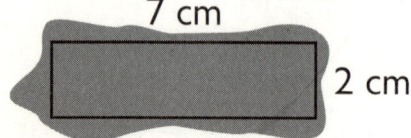
2 cm

☐ square centimeters

10   5 cm
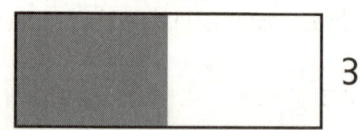
2 cm

☐ square centimeters

Math Explorations and Applications Level 3

LESSON 47 PRACTICE

Name _____

Multiply.

1. 7 × 2 = ☐
2. 3 × 4 = ☐
3. 1 × 6 = ☐
4. 2 × 4 = ☐
5. 6 × 3 = ☐
6. 5 × 2 = ☐
7. 4 × 5 = ☐
8. 2 × 6 = ☐
9. 3 × 7 = ☐
10. 4 × 4 = ☐

Solve these problems.

Mrs. Hermosa bought three packages of meat. The weight of each package was between 3 and 4 pounds.

11. Can Mrs. Hermosa have 7 pounds of meat all together? _____

12. Can Mrs. Hermosa have 10 pounds of meat all together? _____

13. What is the greatest number of pounds of meat Mrs. Hermosa might have? _____

14. What is the least number of pounds of meat Mrs. Hermosa might have? _____

LESSON 48 PRACTICE

Name _____

Multiply.

1. $5 \times 10 =$ ☐
2. $4 \times 6 =$ ☐
3. $7 \times 5 =$ ☐
4. $8 \times 4 =$ ☐
5. $6 \times 3 =$ ☐
6. $10 \times 2 =$ ☐
7. $6 \times 5 =$ ☐
8. $8 \times 6 =$ ☐
9. $3 \times 7 =$ ☐
10. $4 \times 2 =$ ☐

Solve these problems.

Tomas has nine nickels. He wants to buy a toy truck that costs 85¢.

11. How much money does Tomas have? _____

12. How much more money does he need to buy the truck? _____

At the farmers' market an apple costs 6¢ and a pear costs 8¢.

13. How much do four apples cost? _____

14. How much do five pears cost? _____

15. How much do three apples and three pears cost? _____

48 • Math Explorations and Applications Level 3

LESSON 49 PRACTICE

Name _____

Fill in each blank.

1. $7 \times 6 = \boxed{}$
2. $\boxed{} \times 8 = 56$
3. $9 \times 4 = \boxed{}$
4. $\boxed{} \times 4 = 32$
5. $6 \times \boxed{} = 54$
6. $6 \times 6 = \boxed{}$
7. $3 \times \boxed{} = 21$
8. $6 \times 8 = \boxed{}$
9. $\boxed{} \times 7 = 35$
10. $5 \times \boxed{} = 40$

Think about each problem. Then write which number sentence shows you the answer.

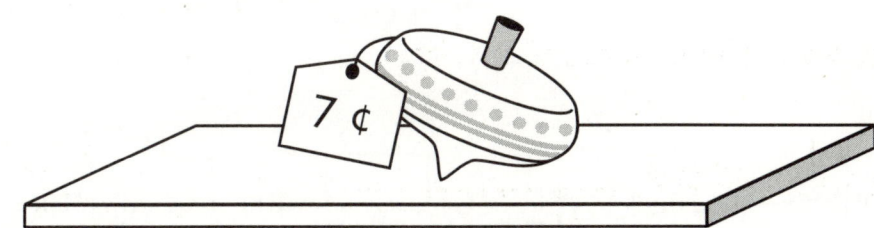

11. One top costs 7¢. How much will six tops cost?

    a. $6 \times 7 = 42$ **b.** $6 + 7 = 13$

12. Marcy wants to buy 24 bottles of juice. Each package has six bottles. How many packages must she buy?

    a. $24 - 6 = 16$ **b.** $4 \times 6 = 24$ $\boxed{}$

Math Explorations and Applications Level 3 • 49

LESSON 50 PRACTICE

Name _____

Multiply.

① 10
 × 5

② 6
 × 7

③ 6
 × 9

④ 3
 × 9

⑤ 8
 × 4

⑥ 9
 × 6

⑦ 4
 × 8

⑧ 9
 × 3

⑨ 8
 × 9

⑩ 7
 × 6

What is the area?

⑪ 4 cm
 6 cm

☐ square centimeters

⑫ 6 cm
 4 cm

☐ square centimeters

⑬ 3 cm
 2 cm

☐ square centimeters

⑭ 2 cm
 3 cm

☐ square centimeters

Solve these problems.

⑮ Mike has eight nickels. How much money does he have?

_____

⑯ Patty has four dimes. How much money does she have?

_____

50 • *Math Explorations and Applications* Level 3

LESSON 51 PRACTICE

Name _____

Billy dreamed about a money machine that produced a $5 bill every hour.

Fill in the chart.

	Number of Hours	Amount of Money			Number of Hours	Amount of Money
❶	1	$		❻	6	$
❷	2	$		❼	7	$
❸	3	$		❽	8	$
❹	4	$		❾	9	$
❺	5	$		❿	10	$

Billy's sister Bridget dreamed about a machine that produced four times as many items as were put into the machine.

Fill in the chart.

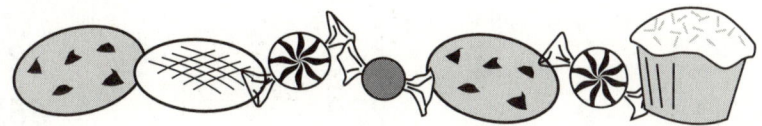

	In		Out
⓫	3 juice boxes	3 × 4	
⓬	6 cookies	6 × 4	
⓭	8 puppies	8 × 4	
⓮	5 apples	5 × 4	
⓯	9 kittens	9 × 4	
⓰	4 dolls	4 × 4	

LESSON 52 PRACTICE

Name _____

Multiply.

1. $85 \times 10 =$ _____
2. $98 \times 10 =$ _____
3. $52 \times 10 =$ _____
4. $10 \times 17 =$ _____
5. $4 \times 10 =$ _____
6. $10 \times 21 =$ _____
7. $10 \times 33 =$ _____
8. $69 \times 10 =$ _____
9. $12 \times 10 =$ _____
10. $10 \times 45 =$ _____
11. $100 \times 10 =$ _____
12. $6 \times 10 =$ _____
13. $10 \times 39 =$ _____
14. $49 \times 10 =$ _____
15. $195 \times 10 =$ _____
16. $234 \times 10 =$ _____
17. $10 \times 3 =$ _____
18. $999 \times 10 =$ _____

Solve. Watch the signs.

19. 48
    + 22

20. 329
    − 148

21. 638
    − 229

22. 2347
    + 6653

23. 500
    − 350

24. 468
    − 395

25. 486
    + 973

26. 670
    + 830

LESSON 53 PRACTICE

Name _____

Multiply.

1. 10 × 14 = _____
2. 20 × 100 = _____
3. 26 × 100 = _____
4. 10 × 85 = _____
5. 10 × 81 = _____
6. 7 × 1000 = _____
7. 1000 × 9 = _____
8. 1000 × 2 = _____
9. 74 × 100 = _____
10. 6 × 1000 = _____
11. 3 × 1000 = _____
12. 100 × 5 = _____
13. 10 × 842 = _____
14. 10 × 750 = _____
15. 50 × 100 = _____
16. 10 × 1000 = _____
17. 4 × 10 = _____
18. 10 × 90 = _____
19. 1000 × 4 = _____
20. 82 × 100 = _____

Solve these problems.

21. Patrick has 16 $10 bills. Does he have enough money to buy the sweater? _____

22. The coffee shop has 39 boxes of mugs. Each contains ten mugs. Are there enough mugs for 400 people? _____

LESSON 54 PRACTICE

Name _____

Multiply.

① 8 × 2 = _____   ② 6 × 2 = _____

③ 0 × 5 = _____   ④ 0 × 0 = _____

⑤ 4 × 1 = _____   ⑥ 1 × 1 = _____

⑦ 10 × 6 = _____   ⑧ 10 × 5 = _____

⑨ 2 × 2 = _____   ⑩ 2 × 3 = _____

⑪ 1 × 9 = _____   ⑫ 10 × 10 = _____

⑬ 4   ⑭ 1   ⑮ 10   ⑯ 2   ⑰ 2
  × 2   × 3   × 2   × 5   × 1

⑱ 4   ⑲ 10   ⑳ 9   ㉑ 10   ㉒ 7
  × 0   × 0   × 2   × 1   × 2

Solve these problems.

㉓ If it takes three oranges to make one glass of orange juice, how many oranges would you need to make one glass of orange juice for yourself and one for a friend? _____

㉔ Pretzels usually cost 10¢ each. Today they are three for a quarter. How much money will you save if you buy three pretzels? _____

54 • *Math Explorations and Applications* Level 3

LESSON 55 PRACTICE

Name _____

Multiply.

① 3 × 3 = _____   ② 10 × 3 = _____
③ 5 × 4 = _____   ④ 5 × 5 = _____
⑤ 7 × 3 = _____   ⑥ 9 × 5 = _____
⑦ 6 × 3 = _____   ⑧ 3 × 4 = _____
⑨ 5 × 2 = _____   ⑩ 3 × 8 = _____
⑪ 7 × 5 = _____   ⑫ 5 × 1 = _____

⑬ 3 × 10   ⑭ 5 × 3   ⑮ 5 × 6   ⑯ 3 × 2

⑰ 5 × 8   ⑱ 3 × 0   ⑲ 5 × 0   ⑳ 10 × 5

㉑ 9 × 3   ㉒ 3 × 1   ㉓ 4 × 5   ㉔ 8 × 3

Math Explorations and Applications Level 3

LESSON 56 PRACTICE

Name _____

Multiply. Work down the page.

1. $10 \times 2 =$ _____
2. $9 \times 2 =$ _____

3. $10 \times 4 =$ _____
4. $9 \times 4 =$ _____

5. $10 \times 7 =$ _____
6. $9 \times 7 =$ _____

7. $10 \times 5 =$ _____
8. $9 \times 5 =$ _____

9. $10 \times 8 =$ _____
10. $9 \times 8 =$ _____

11. $10 \times 6 =$ _____
12. $9 \times 6 =$ _____

13. $10 \times 3 =$ _____
14. $9 \times 3 =$ _____

15. $10 \times 9 =$ _____
16. $9 \times 9 =$ _____

17. $10 \times 1 =$ _____
18. $9 \times 1 =$ _____

19. $10 \times 10 =$ _____
20. $9 \times 10 =$ _____

Multiply.

21. $5 \\ \underline{\times 9}$
22. $6 \\ \underline{\times 5}$
23. $7 \\ \underline{\times 2}$
24. $2 \\ \underline{\times 9}$

LESSON 57 PRACTICE

Name _____

Multiply. Work down the page.

1. $2 \times 7 = $ _____
2. $4 \times 7 = $ _____

3. $2 \times 3 = $ _____
4. $4 \times 3 = $ _____

5. $2 \times 5 = $ _____
6. $4 \times 5 = $ _____

7. $2 \times 6 = $ _____
8. $4 \times 6 = $ _____

9. $2 \times 9 = $ _____
10. $4 \times 9 = $ _____

11. $2 \times 2 = $ _____
12. $4 \times 2 = $ _____

13. $4 \times 4 = $ _____
14. $8 \times 4 = $ _____

15. $4 \times 8 = $ _____
16. $8 \times 8 = $ _____

17. $4 \times 10 = $ _____
18. $8 \times 10 = $ _____

19. $4 \times 1 = $ _____
20. $8 \times 1 = $ _____

Multiply.

21. $\begin{array}{r} 8 \\ \times\, 2 \\ \hline \end{array}$

22. $\begin{array}{r} 8 \\ \times\, 5 \\ \hline \end{array}$

23. $\begin{array}{r} 3 \\ \times\, 8 \\ \hline \end{array}$

24. $\begin{array}{r} 8 \\ \times\, 7 \\ \hline \end{array}$

Math Explorations and Applications Level 3

LESSON 58 PRACTICE

Name _____

Multiply.

1. $8 \times 8 =$ _____
2. $9 \times 3 =$ _____
3. $5 \times 6 =$ _____
4. $2 \times 7 =$ _____
5. $4 \times 9 =$ _____
6. $6 \times 2 =$ _____
7. $5 \times 3 =$ _____
8. $9 \times 7 =$ _____
9. $4 \times 8 =$ _____
10. $3 \times 5 =$ _____
11. $4 \times 10 =$ _____
12. $10 \times 8 =$ _____
13. $4 \times 1 =$ _____
14. $8 \times 3 =$ _____
15. $3 \times 3 =$ _____
16. $8 \times 7 =$ _____

17. 1 × 5
18. 2 × 8
19. 7 × 6
20. 4 × 4

21. 2 × 6
22. 5 × 5
23. 9 × 9
24. 5 × 8

25. 8 × 6
26. 3 × 4
27. 5 × 9
28. 10 × 5

PRACTICE   Name _____

Multiply. Work down the page.

1. 3 × 3 = _____
2. 6 × 3 = _____
3. 3 × 5 = _____
4. 6 × 5 = _____
5. 3 × 7 = _____
6. 6 × 7 = _____
7. 3 × 4 = _____
8. 6 × 4 = _____
9. 3 × 9 = _____
10. 6 × 9 = _____
11. 3 × 2 = _____

12. 6 × 2 = _____
13. 3 × 6 = _____
14. 6 × 6 = _____
15. 3 × 10 = _____
16. 6 × 10 = _____
17. 3 × 1 = _____
18. 6 × 1 = _____
19. 3 × 8 = _____
20. 6 × 8 = _____

Solve these problems.

Carlos is reading a book that has 56 pages.
He is planning to read six pages per day.

21. How many pages will he read after two days? _____

22. How many pages will he read after five days? _____

23. How many days will it take him to read 42 pages? _____

24. Will he finish the book at the end of nine days? If not, how many pages will be left? _____

LESSON 60 PRACTICE

Name _____

What is the area? Write the number of square centimeters.

1. 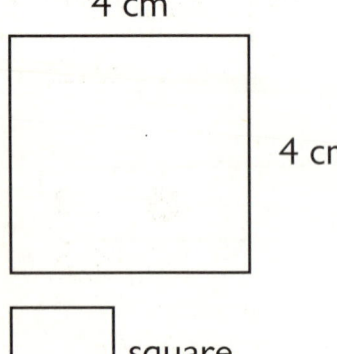 4 cm / 4 cm — ☐ square centimeters

2. 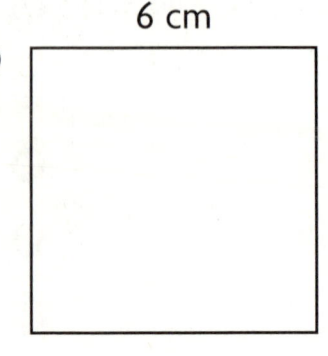 6 cm / 6 cm — ☐ square centimeters

3. 3 cm / 3 cm — ☐ square centimeters

Solve. Watch the signs.

4. 20 − 10 = ☐
5. 16 − 7 = ☐
6. 7 + 8 = ☐
7. 8 + 4 = ☐
8. 13 − 6 = ☐
9. 10 − 3 = ☐
10. 6 + 5 = ☐
11. 8 + 6 = ☐

 **Solve these problems.**

12. The Rams scored five touchdowns. Each touchdown is 6 points. How many points did the Rams score? _____

13. The Mustangs scored two touchdowns and four field goals. Each touchdown is 6 points and each field goal is 3 points. How many points did the Mustangs score? _____

14. Who won? _____

15. By how much? _____

60 • Math Explorations and Applications Level 3

LESSON 61 PRACTICE

Name _____

Multiply.

1) 5
   × 5

2) 7
   × 6

3) 5
   × 7

4) 4
   × 4

5) 7
   × 0

6) 2
   × 2

7) 7
   × 9

8) 3
   × 3

9) 7 × 3 = _____

10) 7 × 7 = _____

11) 7 × 8 = _____

12) 7 × 1 = _____

13) 6 × 6 = _____

14) 8 × 8 = _____

15) 7 × 4 = _____

16) 7 × 5 = _____

17) 9 × 9 = _____

18) 7 × 10 = _____

19) 10 × 10 = _____

20) 0 × 0 = _____

 **Solve these problems.**

21) There are seven children on the playground. Each child has a pair of mittens. How many mittens do the children have all together? _____

22) Each child also has a scarf. How many scarves do they have all together? _____

LESSON 62 PRACTICE

Name _____

Multiply.

1. $6 \times 5 =$ _____
2. $9 \times 3 =$ _____
3. $3 \times 6 =$ _____
4. $6 \times 9 =$ _____
5. $8 \times 2 =$ _____
6. $7 \times 8 =$ _____
7. $9 \times 4 =$ _____
8. $9 \times 7 =$ _____
9. $8 \times 8 =$ _____
10. $4 \times 3 =$ _____
11. $6 \times 4 =$ _____
12. $8 \times 3 =$ _____
13. $2 \times 9 =$ _____
14. $7 \times 6 =$ _____
15. $5 \times 4 =$ _____
16. $8 \times 5 =$ _____

17. 6 × 8
18. 3 × 7
19. 7 × 4
20. 4 × 8

21. 7 × 7
22. 9 × 9
23. 7 × 5
24. 1 × 1

25. 2 × 4
26. 3 × 2
27. 8 × 3
28. 10 × 9

62 • Math Explorations and Applications Level 3

LESSON 63 PRACTICE

Name _____

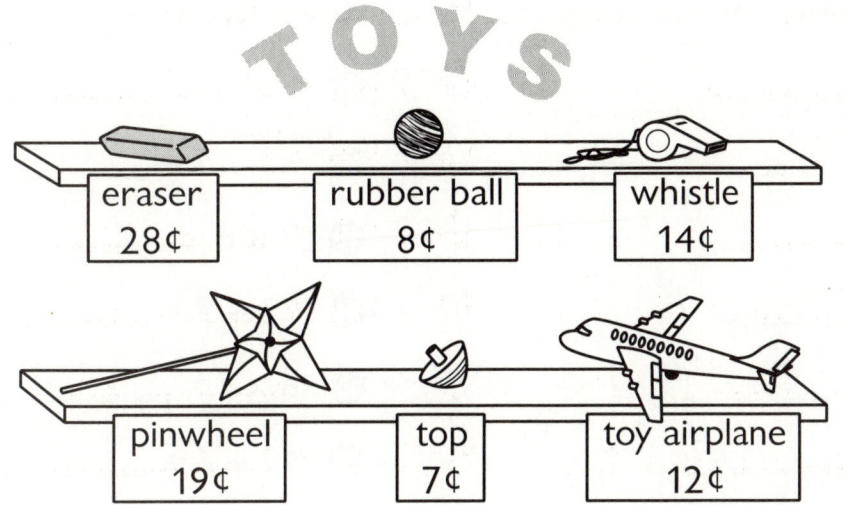

 **Solve these problems.**

① How much will six tops cost? _____

② How much will two erasers cost? _____

③ Maria has 40¢. How many pinwheels can she buy? _____

④ Peter has eight dimes. How much money is that in cents? _____

⑤ Sam has 25¢. Can he buy two toy airplanes? _____

⑥ How much will eight rubber balls cost? _____

⑦ Lucy has five nickels. Can she buy two whistles? _____

⑧ Bobby has nine nickels. How much money is that in cents? _____

Math Explorations and Applications Level 3

LESSON 64 PRACTICE

Name _____

Solve these problems. Watch the signs. Work down the page.

① 10 × 4 = _____

② 40 ÷ 10 = _____

③ 3 × 6 = _____

④ 18 ÷ 3 = _____

⑤ 7 × 8 = _____

⑥ 56 ÷ 7 = _____

⑦ 2 × 9 = _____

⑧ 18 ÷ 2 = _____

⑨ 4 × 8 = _____

⑩ 32 ÷ 4 = _____

⑪ 5 × 7 = _____

⑫ 35 ÷ 5 = _____

⑬ 9 × 8 = _____

⑭ 72 ÷ 9 = _____

⑮ 6 × 7 = _____

⑯ 42 ÷ 6 = _____

⑰ 8 × 3 = _____

⑱ 24 ÷ 8 = _____

⑲ 1 × 2 = _____

⑳ 2 ÷ 1 = _____

Solve these problems.

㉑ Jamal has 50¢. He only has dimes. How many dimes does Jamal have?

50 ÷ 10 = _____

㉒ There are 30 stickers and five students. How many stickers are there for each student?

30 ÷ 5 = _____

㉓ Mrs. Dalton passed out three seeds to each student. There are 27 seeds. How many students are there?

27 ÷ 3 = _____

㉔ There are 12 eggs in a carton. There are two rows. How many eggs are in each row?

12 ÷ 2 = _____

64 • Math Explorations and Applications Level 3

LESSON 65 PRACTICE

Name _____

 **Solve. Watch the signs.**

① 18 ÷ 2 = _____   ② 30 ÷ 5 = _____
③ 10 ÷ 5 = _____   ④ 9 × 3 = _____
⑤ 12 ÷ 4 = _____   ⑥ 24 ÷ 4 = _____
⑦ 3 × 1 = _____   ⑧ 16 ÷ 2 = _____
⑨ 15 ÷ 3 = _____   ⑩ 10 ÷ 1 = _____
⑪ 14 ÷ 2 = _____   ⑫ 27 ÷ 3 = _____
⑬ 9 × _____ = 18   ⑭ _____ × 6 = 24
⑮ _____ × 5 = 10   ⑯ 8 × 2 = _____

⑰ 1)5̄   ⑱ 4)2̄0̄   ⑲ 2)6̄   ⑳ 5)2̄5̄

㉑ 3)2̄4̄   ㉒ 5)2̄0̄   ㉓ 2)4̄   ㉔ 4)8̄

㉕ 4)4̄   ㉖ 2)1̄2̄   ㉗ 5)4̄5̄   ㉘ 3)2̄1̄

LESSON 66 PRACTICE

Name _____

Solve. Look for connections that may help you.

1. $9 \times 5 =$ _____
2. $6 \times 8 =$ _____
3. $7 \times 9 =$ _____
4. $36 \div 6 =$ _____
5. $45 \div 9 =$ _____
6. $6 \times 4 =$ _____
7. $3 \times 9 =$ _____
8. $72 \div 8 =$ _____
9. $48 \div 6 =$ _____
10. $8 \times 5 =$ _____
11. $5 \times 3 =$ _____
12. $6 \times 6 =$ _____
13. $4 \times 8 =$ _____
14. $8 \times 9 =$ _____
15. $15 \div 5 =$ _____
16. $63 \div 7 =$ _____
17. $24 \div 4 =$ _____
18. $40 \div 8 =$ _____
19. $32 \div 4 =$ _____
20. $27 \div 9 =$ _____
21. $70 \div 10 =$ _____
22. $9 \times 6 =$ _____
23. $8 \times 7 =$ _____
24. $6 \times 3 =$ _____
25. $7 \times 10 =$ _____
26. $5 \times 4 =$ _____
27. $20 \div 4 =$ _____
28. $56 \div 8 =$ _____
29. $18 \div 3 =$ _____
30. $54 \div 6 =$ _____

LESSON 67 PRACTICE

Name _____

Solve.

1. $8 \times \square = 24$
2. $\square \times 3 = 9$
3. $4 \times \square = 16$
4. $\square \times 6 = 18$
5. $3 \times \square = 6$
6. $\square \times 4 = 8$
7. $5 \times \square = 20$
8. $\square \times 9 = 36$
9. $10 \times \square = 30$
10. $\square \times 7 = 14$
11. $7 \times \square = 35$
12. $\square \times 2 = 4$
13. $2 \times \square = 8$
14. $\square \times 8 = 40$
15. $6 \times \square = 12$
16. $\square \times 5 = 15$
17. $1 \times \square = 4$
18. $\square \times 1 = 2$
19. $9 \times \square = 27$
20. $\square \times 4 = 0$
21. $2 \times \square = 10$
22. $\square \times 3 = 3$
23. $4 \times \square = 12$
24. $\square \times 6 = 24$

Solve this problem.

25. Tickets for the air and space museum cost $4 for adults and $3 for students. A group of students went to the museum with one adult. They paid $22 for tickets. How many students were in the group? _____

LESSON 68 PRACTICE

Name _____

Solve. Watch the signs. Work down the page.

1. $4 \times \square = 20$
2. $20 \div 4 = $ _____

3. $7 \times \square = 56$
4. $56 \div 7 = $ _____

5. $\square \times 8 = 72$
6. $72 \div 8 = $ _____

7. $3 \times \square = 27$
8. $27 \div 3 = $ _____

9. $\square \times 2 = 6$
10. $6 \div 2 = $ _____

11. $\square \times 4 = 28$
12. $28 \div 7 = $ _____

13. $5 \times \square = 30$
14. $30 \div 5 = $ _____

15. $1 \times \square = 7$
16. $7 \div 1 = $ _____

17. $\square \times 6 = 48$
18. $48 \div 6 = $ _____

19. $9 \times \square = 63$
20. $63 \div 9 = $ _____

21. $\square \times 10 = 80$
22. $80 \div 10 = $ _____

23. $5 \times \square = 40$
24. $40 \div 8 = $ _____

68 • Math Explorations and Applications Level 3

LESSON 69 PRACTICE

Name _____

Divide.

1. 3)5
2. 4)7
3. 3)15
4. 4)15

5. 2)10
6. 2)11
7. 6)20
8. 5)24

9. 5)15
10. 8)16
11. 5)12
12. 3)4

13. 9)20
14. 7)14
15. 7)15
16. 3)8

17. 6)25
18. 5)42
19. 7)65
20. 9)80

21. 9)81
22. 6)17
23. 6)18
24. 6)19

25. 4)25
26. 8)25
27. 4)38
28. 8)38

Math Explorations and Applications Level 3

LESSON 70 PRACTICE

Name _____

Solve. Watch the signs.

①   7
    + 4

②   7
    × 4

③   7
    − 4

④   9
    × 6

⑤   4)28

⑥   9)63

⑦   3)24

⑧   4)24

⑨   537
    + 286

⑩   821
    − 246

⑪   289
    + 378

⑫   605
    − 498

⑬ 15 − 8 = _____

⑭ 36 ÷ 4 = _____

⑮ 9 × 8 = _____

⑯ 12 − 3 = _____

⑰ 14 − 7 = _____

⑱ 10 × 4 = _____

⑲ 15 ÷ 3 = _____

⑳ 8 + 5 = _____

㉑ 9 + 9 = _____

㉒ 21 ÷ 3 = _____

㉓ 6 × 7 = _____

㉔ 8 × 2 = _____

㉕ 63 ÷ 7 = _____

㉖ 30 ÷ 5 = _____

㉗ 7 × 7 = _____

㉘ 13 − 4 = _____

㉙ 6 + 4 = _____

㉚ 8 + 7 = _____

70 • Math Explorations and Applications Level 3

LESSON 71 PRACTICE

Name _____

 **Solve these problems.**

1 The biking club has six teams with four members on each team. How many members are there all together? _____

2 A bag of popcorn costs 8¢. Terry has 35¢. How many bags of popcorn can she buy? _____

3 Bananas cost 9¢ each. How much will six bananas cost? _____

4 Jim was 46 inches tall. Jim grew six inches this year. How tall is he now? _____

5 A school basketball club has 36 players. The coach wants to make four equal teams. How many children will be on each team? _____

6 Polly has 28¢. She buys a gift for her mother. Now she has 6¢. How much did she spend on her mother's gift? _____

7 Gilberto gets 10¢ for each chore he does in a day. Gilberto earned 80¢ in one day. How many chores did Gilberto do? _____

8 Mr. Paul rode his bike 13 kilometers to work and then back home. How far did Mr. Paul ride? _____

Math Explorations and Applications Level 3

LESSON 72 PRACTICE

Name _____

Solve. Watch the signs.

① 8 × 9 = _____

② 56 ÷ 7 = _____

③ 70 ÷ 10 = _____

④ 40 ÷ 8 = _____

⑤ 6 × 7 = _____

⑥ 8 × 8 = _____

⑦ 3 × 9 = _____

⑧ 24 ÷ 6 = _____

⑨ 49 ÷ 7 = _____

⑩ 10 × 9 = _____

⑪ 5 × 6 = _____

⑫ 36 ÷ 9 = _____

⑬ 30 ÷ 5 = _____

⑭ 60 ÷ 6 = _____

⑮ 3 × 10 = _____

⑯ 28 ÷ 7 = _____

⑰ 4 × 9 = _____

⑱ 9 × 9 = _____

⑲ 248 + 672

⑳ 727 − 438

㉑ 409 − 267

㉒ 2750 + 5250

㉓ 800 − 350

㉔ 916 − 587

㉕ 132 + 132 + 268

㉖ 116 + 208 + 201 + 303

LESSON 73 PRACTICE

Name _____

Find a function rule for each set of numbers.

1.
7 → ? → 12
9 → ? → 14
12 → ? → 17
20 → ? → 25

Function rule is _____.

2.
4 → ? → 12
6 → ? → 18
8 → ? → 24
9 → ? → 27

Function rule is _____.

3.
6 → ? → 1
30 → ? → 5
48 → ? → 8
60 → ? → 10

Function rule is _____.

4.
18 → ? → 10
16 → ? → 8
10 → ? → 2
8 → ? → 0

Function rule is _____.

5.
3 → ? → 15
5 → ? → 25
7 → ? → 35
8 → ? → 40

Function rule is _____.

6.
30 → ? → 3
50 → ? → 5
60 → ? → 6
90 → ? → 9

Function rule is _____.

Math Explorations and Applications Level 3 • 73

LESSON 74 PRACTICE

Name _____

Find the value of *n*. Then find the value of *m*.

1. 6 →(−2)→ n →(×4)→ m   n = _____   m = _____

2. 8 →(×3)→ n →(÷4)→ m   n = _____   m = _____

3. 7 →(+7)→ n →(÷2)→ m   n = _____   m = _____

4. 5 →(−2)→ n →(×3)→ m   n = _____   m = _____

5. m ←(×4)← n ←(+5)← 0   n = _____   m = _____

6. 2 →(+52)→ n →(÷6)→ m   n = _____   m = _____

7. m ←(÷5)← n ←(×10)← 4   n = _____   m = _____

74 • *Math Explorations and Applications* Level 3

LESSON 75 PRACTICE

Name _____

 Find the value of *n*. Use inverse arrow operations when necessary.

1. n →(+4)→ m →(×6)→ 36   n = _____

2. n →(×3)→ m →(+3)→ 18   n = _____

3. 7 →(÷7)→ m →(+48)→ n   n = _____

4. 20 ←(+4)← m ←(×2)← n   n = _____

5. n →(×5)→ m →(+50)→ 100   n = _____

6. 27 ←(×9)← m ←(÷5)← n   n = _____

7. 12 →(+5)→ m →(−4)→ n   n = _____

8. n →(×5)→ m →(+8)→ 38   n = _____

9. 37 ←(+13)← m ←(×6)← n   n = _____

Math Explorations and Applications Level 3 • 75

LESSON 76 PRACTICE

Name _____

Use the function rule to solve the problems.

1. If x = 7, what is y? _____
2. If y = 7, what is x? _____
3. If x = 10, what is y? _____
4. If y = 10, what is x? _____

5. If x = 4, what is y? _____
6. If y = 54, what is x? _____
7. If x = 8, what is y? _____
8. If y = 36, what is x? _____

9. If x = 24, what is y? _____
10. If x = 36, what is y? _____
11. If y = 4, what is x? _____
12. If y = 10, what is x? _____

13. If x = 17, what is y? _____
14. If x = 13, what is y? _____
15. If y = 8, what is x? _____
16. If y = 4, what is x? _____

17. If x = 9, what is y? _____
18. If y = 17, what is x? _____
19. If x = 4, what is y? _____
20. If y = 14, what is x? _____

21. If x = 5, what is y? _____
22. If y = 27, what is x? _____
23. If x = 9, what is y? _____
24. If y = 63, what is x? _____

76 • *Math Explorations and Applications* Level 3

LESSON 77 PRACTICE

Name _____

Use the table below to answer each question.

Belt Design	Number of Beads
Bird	3056
Arrow	2288
Lightning	1810
Star	1984

❶ What is the difference between the number of beads needed to make the bird belt and the number needed to make the star belt design? _____

❷ What is the difference between the number of beads needed to make the bird belt and the number needed to make the lightning belt design? _____

❸ What is the difference between the number of beads needed to make the arrow belt and the number needed to make the star belt design? _____

❹ How many beads would be needed to make two of the star belts? _____

❺ How many beads would be needed to make an arrow belt and a lightning belt? _____

Math Explorations and Applications Level 3 • **77**

LESSON 78 PRACTICE

Name _____

Use this code to solve the problems. Then write the riddle for the answer **GEOMETRY**.

A	B	C	D	E	F	G	H	I	J	K	L	M
1	2	3	4	5	6	7	8	9	10	11	12	13

N	O	P	Q	R	S	T	U	V	W	X	Y	Z
14	15	16	17	18	19	20	21	22	23	24	25	26

1. $10 + 13 =$ _____
2. $32 \div 4 =$ _____
3. $5 \div 5 =$ _____
4. $5 \times 4 =$ _____
5. $12 - 8 =$ _____
6. $3 + 6 =$ _____
7. $8 \div 2 =$ _____
8. $10 + 10 =$ _____
9. $56 \div 7 =$ _____
10. $11 - 6 =$ _____
11. $20 - 19 =$ _____
12. $1 \times 3 =$ _____
13. $5 \times 3 =$ _____
14. $9 + 9 =$ _____
15. $2 \times 7 =$ _____
16. $10 + 9 =$ _____
17. $10 \div 10 =$ _____
18. $5 \times 5 =$ _____
19. $20 + 3 =$ _____
20. $64 \div 8 =$ _____
21. $12 - 7 =$ _____
22. $9 + 5 =$ _____
23. $81 \div 9 =$ _____
24. $2 \times 10 =$ _____
25. $21 \div 3 =$ _____
26. $9 \times 2 =$ _____
27. $30 \div 6 =$ _____
28. $11 + 12 =$ _____
29. $7 \times 3 =$ _____
30. $2 \times 8 =$ _____

___ ___ ___ ___   ___ ___ ___   ___ ___ ___   ___ ___ ___ ___ ___
1   2   3   4   5   6   7   8   9   10   11   12   13   14   15

___ ___ ___   ___ ___ ___ ___   ___ ___   ___ ___ ___ ___   ___ ___?
16   17   18   19   20   21   22   23   24   25   26   27   28   29   30

Math Explorations and Applications Level 3

LESSON 79 PRACTICE

Name _____

A third-grade class conducted a survey of its favorite lunch. The results are below.

Favorite Lunch	
	Tally
pizza	涙 涙 (10)
spaghetti	涙 III (8)
peanut butter	IIII (4)
chicken fingers	II (2)

Fill in the pictograph below. Use a circle to represent two children.

Favorite Lunch	
❶ pizza	
❷ spaghetti	
❸ peanut butter	
❹ chicken fingers	

Each ○ represents 2 students.

Favorite Sport Survey	
baseball	○○○○○○○
basketball	○○○
soccer	○ ◐
swimming	○○○○ ◐
tennis	○○ ◐

Each ○ represents 2 students.

Use the pictograph above to answer the questions.

❺ How many students were surveyed? _____

❻ Which sport did the most students say was their favorite? _____

❼ Which sport did the least students say was their favorite? _____

Math Explorations and Applications Level 3 • 79

LESSON 80 PRACTICE

Name _____

A third-grade class conducted a survey of its favorite color. The results are below.

Favorite Color		
	Tally	
red	⊬⊬⊬ I	(6)
blue	⊬⊬⊬ III	(8)
green	III	(3)
purple	⊬⊬⊬	(5)
yellow	II	(2)

Fill in the bar graph below using the matching color.

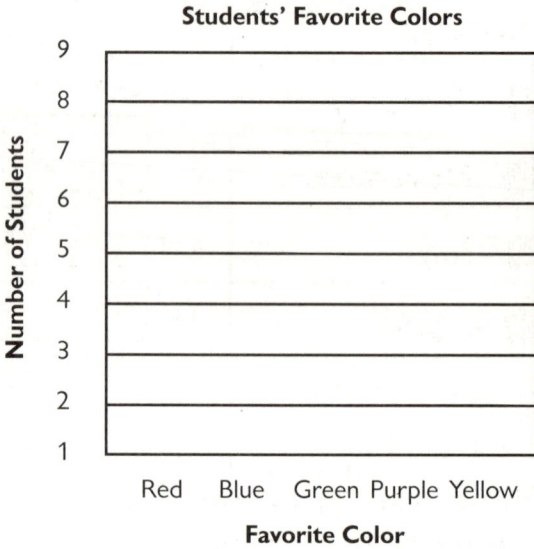

Use the following bar graph to answer the questions.

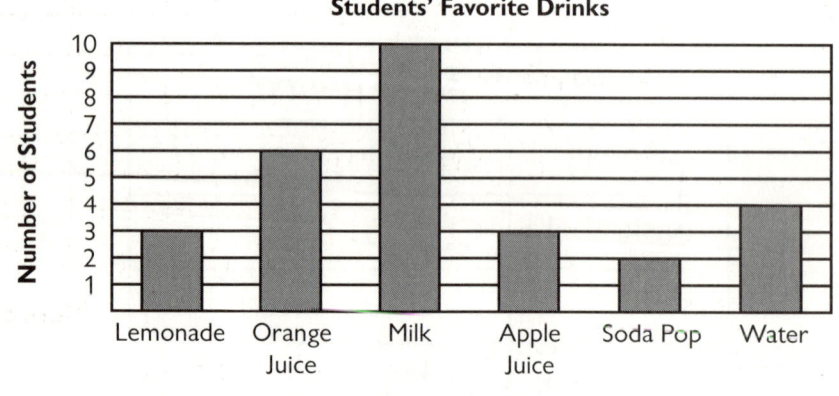

❶ How many students were surveyed? _____

❷ Which drink did the most students say was their favorite? _____

❸ Which drink did the least students say was their favorite? _____

❹ How many students said apple juice was their favorite? _____

❺ How many more students prefer milk than orange juice? _____

❻ What drink is preferred less than lemonade? _____

80 • *Math Explorations and Applications* Level 3

LESSON 81 PRACTICE

Name _____

Use the graph to answer these questions.

What were the sales in these months?

1. February _____
2. November _____
3. July _____
4. April _____

What was the increase in sales during these months?

5. from January to February _____
6. from October to December _____
7. from March to April _____
8. from August to September _____

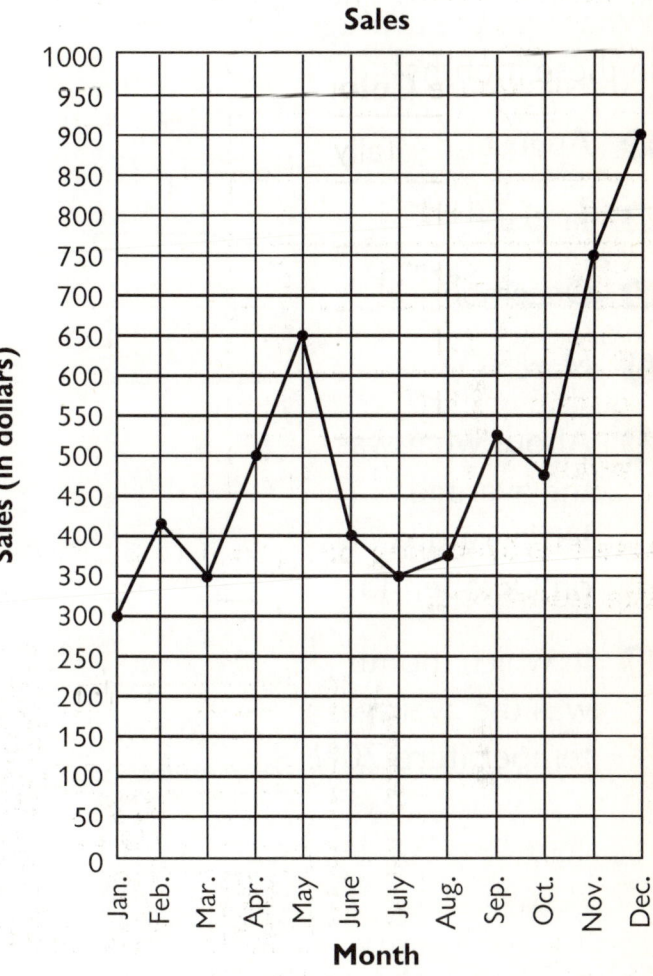

LESSON 82 PRACTICE

Name _____

Use the graph to answer these questions.

What was the average temperature in these months?

1. August _____
2. January _____
3. December _____
4. March _____
5. About what was the average temperature on October 15? _____
6. In which month was the average temperature 70°? _____

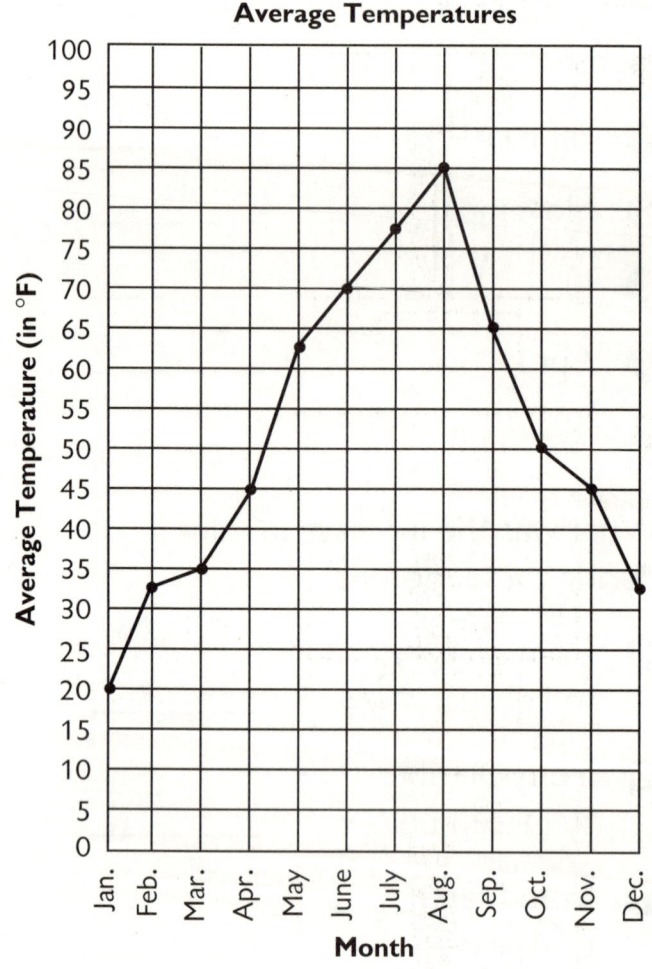

Solve. Watch the signs.

7. 9
    × 6

8. 5
    + 7

9. 9
    − 3

10. 5
    × 4

11. 7
    + 6

12. 602
    − 186

13. 231
    − 74

14. 612
    145
    + 75

15. 824
    102
    214
    + 73

82 • *Math Explorations and Applications* Level 3

LESSON 83 PRACTICE

Name _____

Write the temperature shown on each Fahrenheit thermometer.

❶ 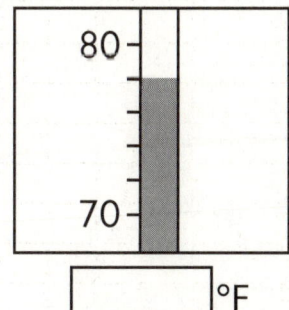 ____°F

❷ 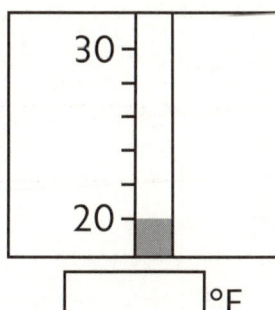 ____°F

❸ 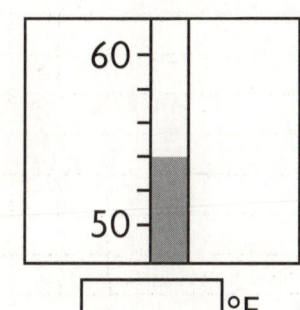 ____°F

❹ 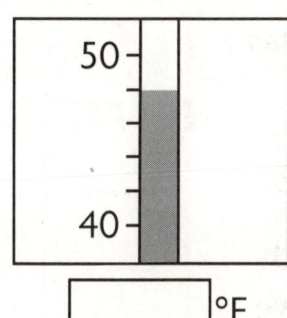 ____°F

❺ 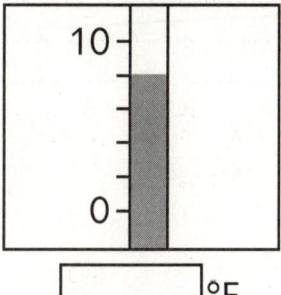 ____°F

❻ 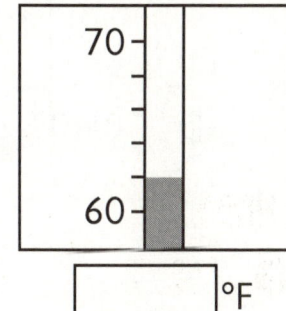 ____°F

❼ 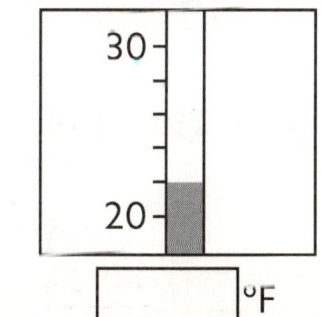 ____°F

❽ 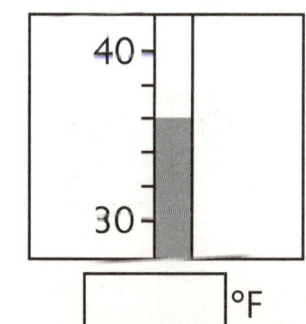 ____°F

LESSON 84 PRACTICE

Name _____

Solve. Watch the signs.

① $0 \times 9 =$ _____

② $56 \div 7 =$ _____

③ $7 \times 5 =$ _____

④ $40 \div 8 =$ _____

⑤ $6 \times 8 =$ _____

⑥ $24 \div 6 =$ _____

⑦ $3 \times 9 =$ _____

⑧ $36 \div 9 =$ _____

⑨ $7 \times 7 =$ _____

⑩ $8 \div 2 =$ _____

⑪ $5 \times 6 =$ _____

⑫ $81 \div 9 =$ _____

⑬ 324 + 176

⑭ 525 − 499

⑮ 839 − 473

⑯ 250 + 650

Divide.

⑰ $6\overline{)19}$

⑱ $8\overline{)40}$

⑲ $2\overline{)11}$

⑳ $5\overline{)45}$

㉑ $4\overline{)36}$

㉒ $3\overline{)18}$

㉓ $7\overline{)38}$

㉔ $6\overline{)36}$

LESSON 85 PRACTICE

Name _____

Units of Measure

There are 100 centimeters in 1 meter.
100 cm = 1 m
There are 1000 meters in 1 kilometer.
1000 m = 1 km

Units of Weight

There are 1000 grams in 1 kilogram.
1000 g = 1 kg

Solve.

① 1 kg = ☐ g   ② 1 m = ☐ cm   ③ 1 km = ☐ m

④ 4 kg = ☐ g   ⑤ 6 m = ☐ cm   ⑥ 7 km = ☐ m

⑦ 9 km = ☐ m   ⑧ 2 kg = ☐ g   ⑨ 3 m = ☐ cm

⑩ ☐ m = 6 km   ⑪ ☐ g = 8 kg   ⑫ ☐ cm = 5 m

Choose the number that seems most reasonable.

⑬  weighs about _____ kg. (2, 20, 200)

⑭  is about _____ cm tall. (5, 50, 500)

⑮  weighs about _____ kg. (6, 60, 600)

⑯  weighs about _____ kg. (5, 50, 500)

⑰  weighs about _____ grams. (5, 50, 500)

LESSON 86 PRACTICE

Name _____

Estimate the length. Then measure to check.

①

_____ centimeters

②

_____ centimeters

③

_____ centimeters

 **Solve these problems.**

④ Mr. Gilliam is 143 centimeters tall. Mrs. Gilliam is 131 centimeters tall. How much taller is Mr. Gilliam than his wife?   _____ centimeters

⑤ Sue weighed 76 kilograms. After three months she weighed 67 kilograms. How much weight did Sue lose?   _____ kilograms

LESSON 87

Name _____

Units of Measure
There are 12 inches in 1 foot.
There are 3 feet in 1 yard.
There are 36 inches in 1 yard.
There are 5280 feet in 1 mile.

Units of Weight
There are 16 ounces in 1 pound.

Solve.

❶ 1 yard = _____ feet

❷ 3 feet = _____ inches

❸ 1 pound = _____ ounces

❹ 4 yards = _____ feet

❺ 2 miles = _____ feet

❻ 3 pounds = _____ ounces

❼ 10 yards = _____ feet

❽ 2 yards = _____ inches

❾ 5 yards = _____ feet

❿ 10 pounds = _____ ounces

⓫ 6 feet = _____ inches

⓬ 1 mile = _____ feet

⓭ 3 yards = _____ inches

⓮ 2 pounds = _____ ounces

Choose the number that seems most reasonable.

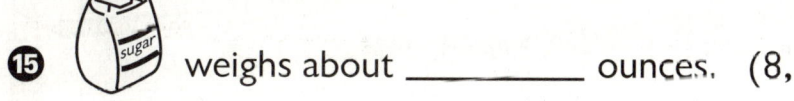

⓯ sugar weighs about _____ ounces. (8, 80, 800)

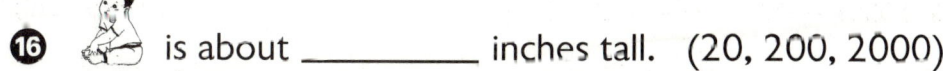

⓰ is about _____ inches tall. (20, 200, 2000)

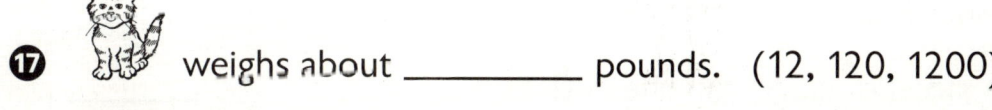

⓱ weighs about _____ pounds. (12, 120, 1200)

⓲ cereal is about _____ yard high. ($\frac{1}{4}$, $\frac{1}{2}$, 1)

LESSON 88 PRACTICE

Name _____

Estimate the length. Then measure to check.

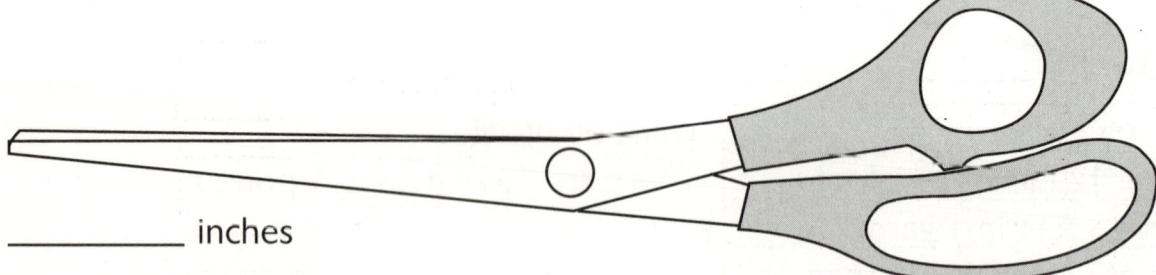

_____ inches

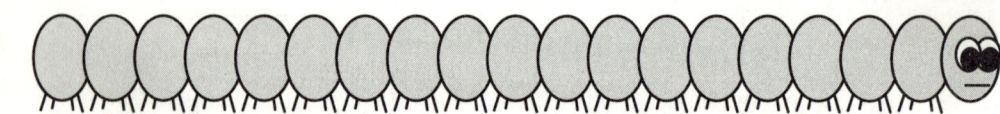

_____ inches

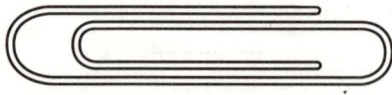

_____ inches

 **Solve these problems.**

④ Mr. Morris and his daughter are baking banana bread. They need 1 pound of walnuts. Each package of walnuts weighs 4 ounces. How many packages should they buy? _____

Toni has a piece of fabric that is 2 yards long. She needs strips of fabric that are 10 inches long.

⑤ How many 10-inch strips of fabric can she cut? _____

⑥ How many inches of fabric will be left over? _____

LESSON 89 PRACTICE

Name _____

Complete the graph of multiples of 3 in red and multiples of 4 in blue.

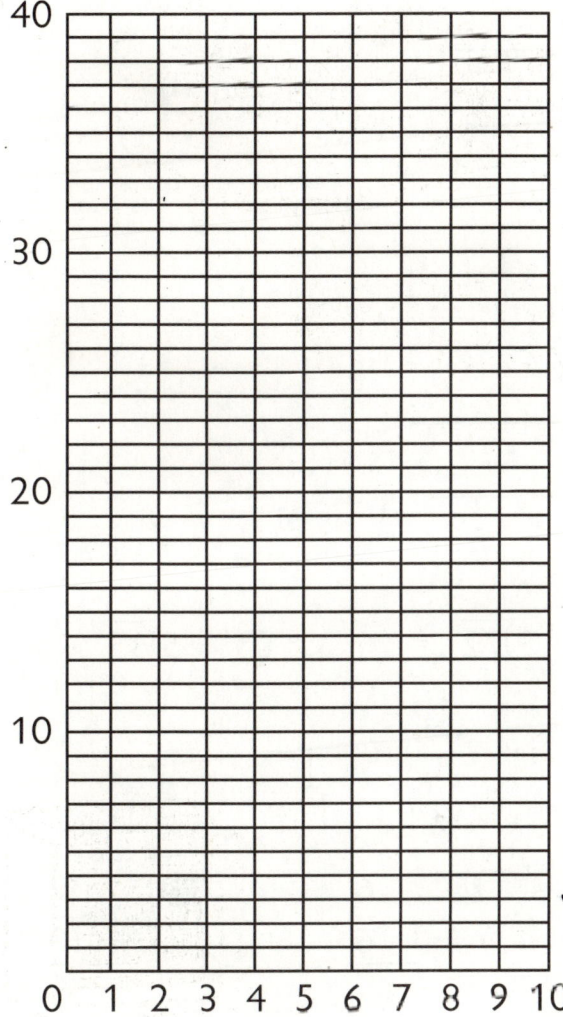

1. $0 \times 3 =$ ☐
2. $2 \times 3 =$ ☐
3. $4 \times 3 =$ ☐
4. $6 \times 3 =$ ☐
5. $8 \times 3 =$ ☐
6. $10 \times 3 =$ ☐
7. $0 \times 4 =$ ☐
8. $1 \times 4 =$ ☐
9. $3 \times 4 =$ ☐
10. $5 \times 4 =$ ☐
11. $7 \times 4 =$ ☐
12. $9 \times 4 =$ ☐
13. $10 \times 4 =$ ☐

Math Explorations and Applications Level 3

LESSON 90 PRACTICE

Name _____

Multiply.

① $4 \times 8 =$ _____   ② $10 \times 9 =$ _____

③ $7 \times 3 =$ _____   ④ $9 \times 5 =$ _____

⑤ $6 \times 7 =$ _____   ⑥ $8 \times 2 =$ _____

Divide.

⑦ $56 \div 8 =$ _____   ⑧ $70 \div 7 =$ _____

⑨ $24 \div 4 =$ _____   ⑩ $30 \div 10 =$ _____

⑪ $40 \div 5 =$ _____   ⑫ $16 \div 2 =$ _____

⑬ $4\overline{)36}$ ⑭ $3\overline{)18}$ ⑮ $9\overline{)72}$ ⑯ $5\overline{)35}$

Solve. Watch the signs.

⑰ $\;\;16$ ⑱ $\;\;8$ ⑲ $\;\;13$ ⑳ $\;\;6$ ㉑ $\;\;9$
$\;\;-\;9$ $\;\;+\;4$ $\;\;-\;7$ $\;\;+\;6$ $\;+\;10$

㉒ $\;\;4$ ㉓ $\;\;7$ ㉔ $\;\;11$ ㉕ $\;\;5$ ㉖ $\;\;5$
$\;+\;6$ $\;+\;8$ $\;-\;4$ $\;-\;5$ $\;+\;5$

90 • Math Explorations and Applications Level 3

PRACTICE Name _____

What is the right sign? Draw <, >, or =.

1. $7 \times 8 \bigcirc 8 \times 4$
2. $4 \times 3 \bigcirc 2 \times 3$
3. $24 \div 3 \bigcirc 24 \div 4$
4. $18 \div 3 \bigcirc 18 \div 2$
5. $9 + 5 \bigcirc 7 + 7$
6. $7 + 5 \bigcirc 6 + 6$
7. $9 \times 4 \bigcirc 6 \times 6$
8. $20 \div 2 \bigcirc 20 \div 4$
9. $11 - 4 \bigcirc 15 - 4$
10. $8 \times 10 \bigcirc 1 \times 1$
11. $6 + 7 \bigcirc 5 + 8$
12. $9 \times 6 \bigcirc 8 \times 7$
13. $12 \div 2 \bigcirc 12 \div 6$
14. $15 \div 3 \bigcirc 16 \div 4$
15. $16 - 8 \bigcirc 14 - 9$
16. $11 - 3 \bigcirc 18 - 10$
17. $5 + 6 \bigcirc 6 + 4$
18. $9 + 4 \bigcirc 7 + 6$
19. $30 \div 10 \bigcirc 30 \div 5$
20. $4 \times 7 \bigcirc 5 \times 6$

LESSON 92 PRACTICE

Name _____

Solve.

1. $8 and 6 dimes = ☐ dimes

2. $2 and 1 dime = ☐ dimes

3. $ ☐ = $11 and 4 dimes

4. 47 dimes = $ ☐ and ☐ dimes

5. 23 dimes = $ ☐ and ☐ dimes

6. $14.20 = $ ☐ and ☐ dimes

7. $ ☐ and ☐ dimes = $7.30

8. $ ☐ = $4 and 5 dimes

9. $3.70 = $ ☐ and ☐ dimes

10. $12.50 = $ ☐ and ☐ dimes

11. $ ☐ and ☐ dimes = $10.80

12. $ ☐ and ☐ dimes = $1.20

13. $9 and 3 dimes = ☐ dimes

14. $1.40 = $ ☐ and ☐ dimes

15. $ ☐ = $5 and 8 dimes

16. $ ☐ and ☐ dimes = $6.90

17. $10 and 7 dimes = ☐ dimes

18. $7.80 = $ ☐ and ☐ dimes

Math Explorations and Applications Level 3

LESSON 93 PRACTICE   Name _____

Solve.

1. 10 dimes = $_____
2. 50 dimes = $_____
3. 100 dimes = $_____
4. 34 dimes = $_____ and _____ dimes
5. 61 dimes = $_____ and _____ dimes
6. 114 dimes = $_____ and _____ dimes
7. $4 and 0 dimes = _____ dimes
8. $3 and 5 dimes = _____ dimes
9. $10 and 2 dimes = _____ dimes
10. $17 and 8 dimes = _____ dimes
11. $1 = _____ dimes
12. $8 = _____ dimes
13. $12 = _____ dimes
14. $4.20 = $_____ and _____ dimes
15. $7.80 = $_____ and _____ dimes
16. $12.10 = $_____ and _____ dimes
17. $5 and 1 dime = $_____
18. $9 and 7 dimes = $_____

LESSON 94 PRACTICE

Name _____

Solve.

① 10 dm = [ ] m

② 40 dm = [ ] m

③ 100 dm = [ ] m

④ 500 dm = [ ] m

⑤ 800 dm = [ ] m

⑥ 1000 dm = [ ] m

⑦ 21 dm = [ ] m and [ ] dm

⑧ 37 dm = [ ] m and [ ] dm

⑨ 103 dm = [ ] m and [ ] dm

⑩ 4 m and 6 dm = [ ] dm

⑪ 9 m and 1 dm = [ ] dm

⑫ 30 m and 5 dm = [ ] dm

⑬ 8.9 m = [ ] m and [ ] dm

⑭ 14.8 m = [ ] m and [ ] dm

⑮ 2.7 m = [ ] m and [ ] dm

⑯ 50.3 m = [ ] m and [ ] dm

⑰ 1 m and 5 dm = [ ] m

⑱ 6 m and 9 dm = [ ] m

94 • *Math Explorations and Applications* Level 3

PRACTICE Name _____

Solve.

① 100 cm = [ ] m
② 400 cm = [ ] m
③ 900 cm = [ ] m
④ 1300 cm = [ ] m
⑤ 1 m = [ ] cm
⑥ 5 m = [ ] cm
⑦ 8 m = [ ] cm
⑧ 14 m = [ ] cm

⑨ 2 m and 35 cm = [ ] cm
⑩ 7 m and 8 cm = [ ] cm
⑪ 4 m and [ ] cm = 479 cm
⑫ 3 m and [ ] cm = 302 cm
⑬ [ ] m and 12 cm = 812 cm
⑭ [ ] m and 68 cm = 168 cm
⑮ 5 m and 10 cm = [ ] cm
⑯ [ ] m and 23 cm = 423 cm
⑰ 9 m and [ ] cm = 907 cm
⑱ 6 m and 52 cm = [ ] cm
⑲ [ ] m and 73 cm = 73 cm
⑳ 2 m and 4 cm = [ ] cm

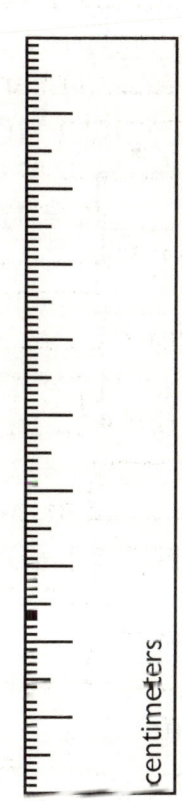

Math Explorations and Applications Level 3 • **95**

LESSON 96 PRACTICE

Name _____

Solve.

① 100¢ = $ ☐

② 500¢ = $ ☐

③ 1200¢ = $ ☐

④ $1 = ☐ ¢

⑤ $6 = ☐ ¢

⑥ $11 = ☐ ¢

⑦ $2 and 81¢ = ☐ ¢

⑧ $9 and 4¢ = ☐ ¢

⑨ $15 and 37¢ = ☐ ¢

⑩ $7 and ☐ ¢ = 739¢

⑪ $1 and ☐ ¢ = 110¢

⑫ $12 and ☐ ¢ = 1212¢

⑬ $10 and ☐ ¢ = 1000¢

⑭ $☐ and 71¢ = 471¢

⑮ $☐ and 25¢ = 325¢

⑯ $☐ and 8¢ = 608¢

⑰ $☐ and ☐ ¢ = 375¢

⑱ $☐ and ☐ ¢ = 803¢

⑲ $☐ and ☐ ¢ = 1522¢

⑳ $☐ and ☐ ¢ = 1701¢

96 • *Math Explorations and Applications* Level 3

 PRACTICE   Name _____

Rewrite to show less than 100¢.

① $2 and 350¢ = $ [ ] and [ ] ¢

② $6 and 125¢ = $ [ ] and [ ] ¢

③ $5 and 542¢ = $ [ ] and [ ] ¢

④ $3 and 200¢ = $ [ ] and [ ] ¢

⑤ $8 and 379¢ = $ [ ] and [ ] ¢

⑥ $1 and 103¢ = $ [ ] and [ ] ¢

⑦ $4 and 162¢ = $ [ ] and [ ] ¢

⑧ $10 and 275¢ = $ [ ] and [ ] ¢

⑨ $7 and 115¢ = $ [ ] and [ ] ¢

⑩ $9 and 206¢ = $ [ ] and [ ] ¢

⑪ $6 and 804¢ = $ [ ] and [ ] ¢

⑫ $3 and 133¢ = $ [ ] and [ ] ¢

PRACTICE   Name _____

Complete each statement.

① There are [ ] hundredths in 1 tenth.

② [ ] dime = 10 cents

③ 1 dm = [ ] cm

④ There are 40 hundredths in [ ] tenths.

⑤ [ ] dimes = 40 cents

⑥ 4 dm = [ ] cm

⑦ There are [ ] hundredths in 9 tenths.

⑧ 9 dimes = [ ] cents

⑨ 9 dm = [ ] cm

⑩ There are [ ] hundredths in 2 tenths.

⑪ [ ] dimes = 20 cents

⑫ 2 dm = [ ] cm

⑬ There are 70 hundredths in [ ] tenths.

⑭ [ ] dimes = 70 cents

⑮ 7 dm = [ ] cm

98 • Math Explorations and Applications Level 3

LESSON 99 PRACTICE

Name _____

What is the right sign? Draw <, >, or =.

1. 2.6 ◯ 2.60
2. 6.7 ◯ 5.9
3. 1.07 ◯ 0.17
4. 0.3 ◯ 0.14
5. 6.30 ◯ 6.4
6. 1.76 ◯ 17.6
7. 0.5 ◯ 0.50
8. 2 ◯ 2.0
9. 1.92 ◯ 2.19
10. 10.1 ◯ 1.01
11. 40.7 ◯ 4.07
12. 0.04 ◯ 0.40
13. 0.1 ◯ 0.01
14. 8.1 ◯ 0.81
15. 8.0 ◯ 0.8
16. 3.75 ◯ 3.8
17. 14.9 ◯ 4.91
18. 1.69 ◯ 1.96
19. 3.6 ◯ 36
20. 4.2 ◯ 4.02
21. 4 ◯ 0.5
22. 0.66 ◯ 0.6

LESSON 100 PRACTICE

Name _____

Add.

①   4.17
     + 2.19

②   6.04
     + 1.87

③   0.15
     + 6.89

④   3.2
     + 4.75

⑤   5.91
     + 0.86

⑥   4.23
     + 2.9

⑦   9.44
     + 0.17

⑧   4.01
     + 5.99

⑨   27.63
     + 42.87

⑩   71.20
     + 8.95

⑪   6.38
     + 17.4

⑫   23.7
     + 2.78

⑬ 7.6 + 8.9 = _____

⑭ 0.6 + 21.7 = _____

⑮ 13.1 + 7.5 = _____

⑯ 3 + 1.72 = _____

⑰ 2.98 + 46.9 = _____

⑱ 8.6 + 1.58 = _____

⑲ 17.5 + 1.75 = _____

⑳ 0.42 + 9 = _____

Solve these problems.

㉑ A pair of shoes costs $34.95. A pair of socks costs $1.29. How much do the shoes and socks cost together? _____

㉒ Phil had $6.75. Then he earned $3.25. How much does he have now? _____

100 • Math Explorations and Applications Level 3

PRACTICE   Name _____

Subtract.

①   8.71   ②   9.27   ③   4.0   ④   8.68
    − 2.65   − 2.8   − 1.75   − 0.9

⑤   5.15   ⑥   6.39   ⑦   7.32   ⑧   86
    − 2   − 0.79   − 0.4   − 1.9

⑨   9.27   ⑩   7.08   ⑪   3.07   ⑫   4.3
    − 6.13   − 6.99   − 1.70   − 2.91

⑬   5.2 − 4.7 = _____   ⑭   11.6 − 8.8 = _____

⑮   10.93 − 10.90 = _____   ⑯   7 − 2.0 = _____

⑰   16.4 − 1.6 = _____   ⑱   12.17 − 5 = _____

⑲   20.4 − 8.75 = _____   ⑳   7.02 − 0.34 = _____

LESSON 102 PRACTICE

Name _____

Solve. Watch the signs. Look for problems that are alike.

① 725
 + 176

② 8.0
 − 4.55

③ 24.3
 + 6.90

④ 90.8
 − 37.2

⑤ 9.08
 − 3.72

⑥ 7.25
 + 1.76

⑦ 3.4
 − 0.71

⑧ 3.40
 − 0.71

⑨ 1.65
 + 7.2

⑩ 500
 − 250

⑪ 800
 − 455

⑫ 50.0
 − 25.0

⑬ 2430
 + 690

⑭ 80.00
 − 45.5

⑮ 72.5
 + 17.6

⑯ 165
 + 720

⑰ 5.0
 − 2.5

⑱ 908
 − 372

⑲ 340
 − 71

⑳ 2.43
 + 0.69

㉑ 19.57
 + 3.20

㉒ 4.73
 − 2.25

㉓ 195
 + 32

㉔ 473
 − 225

102 • Math Explorations and Applications Level 3

LESSON 103 PRACTICE

Name _____

The numbers below give the math test scores of a third-grade class.

78	91	54	67	73	79	82	80	97	43
68	81	67	72	83	59	67	75	85	57
91	45	94	97	64	69	81	72	91	68

❶ What is the lowest score? _____

❷ What is the highest score? _____

❸ What scores appear most often? _____

In the chart below, the number 78 is written as 7 tens and 8 ones.

❹ Use the scores from above to complete the chart.

Tens	Ones
9	
8	
7	8,
6	
5	
4	

❺ Is it now easier to find the lowest, highest, and most common score? _____

❻ Could you now easily put the scores in order from lowest to highest? _____

Math Explorations and Applications Level 3 • 103

LESSON 104 PRACTICE

Name _____

 **Solve these problems.**

1 Each brownie costs 35¢. How much do four brownies cost? _____

2 Katie received $10 as a gift. She spent some money for a movie and a snack. She has $2.52 left. How much did Katie spend? _____

3 Eduardo has $20. Can he afford to buy the CD and music book? _____

4 If Eduardo buys a cassette tape, how much change would he get from his $20? _____

5 Jessica has $45. Can she afford to buy the radio and cassette tape? _____

6 If Jessica wants to buy the keyboard, how much more money would she need? _____

LESSON 105 PRACTICE

Name _____

Solve these problems.

1 Mrs. Richards is painting her kitchen. She needs to buy three more gallons of paint. Each gallon of paint costs $13.79. How much will the paint cost? _____

2 If Mrs. Richards gives the salesperson $50, how much change will she get? _____

Each week Larry jogs 6.2 miles on Monday, 4.7 miles on Wednesday, and 7.5 miles on Friday.

3 How far does Larry jog each week? _____

4 How much farther does Larry jog on Friday than on Monday? _____

5 How many miles will Larry jog in two weeks? _____

6 If Larry jogs only on Monday and Wednesday, how many miles will he jog? _____

Bill's mother deposited $8.50 in his savings account. Bill gets 50¢ allowance each week, which he then deposits in his savings account. These are his account balances for the past three weeks.

$9.00 $9.50 $10.00

7 Bill would like to know how much money he will have in his savings account three weeks from now. Continue the pattern for three more weeks.

$9.00 $9.50 $10.00   _____ _____ _____

8 How much money will Bill have three weeks from now? _____

LESSON 106 PRACTICE

Name _____

Solve. Watch the signs.

①   16.24
     − 9.3

②   8.9
     + 4.1

③   13.5
     − 7.86

④   6.47
     + 8.64

⑤   4.7
     + 10.53

⑥   7.13
     + 8.89

⑦   11.21
     − 4.6

⑧   9.37
     − 8.59

⑨ 6.4 + 7.32 = _____

⑩ 3.76 − 1.8 = _____

⑪ 7.3 − 1.45 = _____

⑫ 4.53 − 3.67 = _____

⑬ 5.25 + 1.75 = _____

⑭ 1.9 + 3.8 = _____

⑮ 4.47 + 1.3 = _____

⑯ 3.7 − 1.25 = _____

Solve these problems.

⑰ Maxine rode her bike 4.5 miles on Saturday and 6.8 miles on Sunday. How far did she ride over the weekend? _____

⑱ Today Pete walked 1.75 miles to school, 0.8 miles to his friend's house, and 2.1 miles back home. How far did Pete walk all together today? _____

LESSON 107 PRACTICE

Name _____

What fraction of each figure is shaded?

 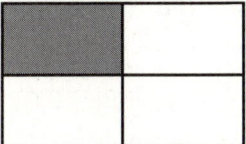    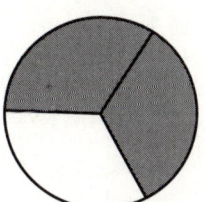 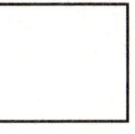

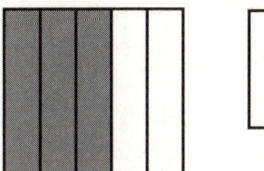    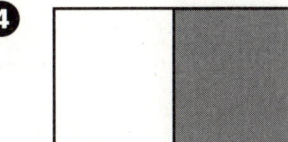 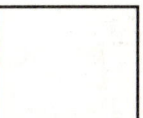

Shade each figure for the given fraction.

5 Color $\frac{1}{3}$ of the figure.

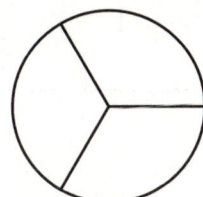

6 Color $\frac{1}{4}$ of the figure.

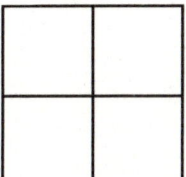

7 Color $\frac{3}{4}$ of the figure.

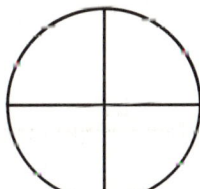

8 Color $\frac{1}{2}$ of the figure.

Math Explorations and Applications Level 3 • **107**

LESSON 108 PRACTICE

Name _____

Shade each figure for the given fraction.

1 Color $\frac{1}{2}$ of the circle.

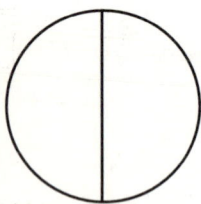

2 Color $\frac{2}{2}$ of the circle.

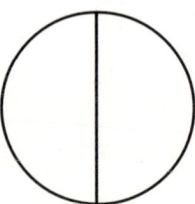

3 Color $\frac{1}{3}$ of the square.

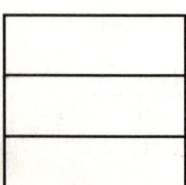

4 Color $\frac{2}{3}$ of the square.

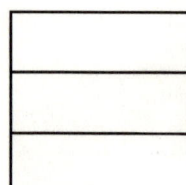

5 Color $\frac{1}{4}$ of the rectangle.

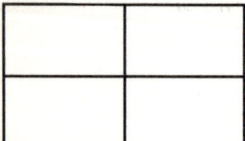

6 Color $\frac{3}{4}$ of the rectangle.

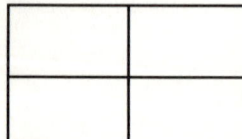

7 Color $\frac{2}{5}$ of the circle.

8 Color $\frac{4}{5}$ of the square.

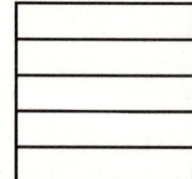

Math Explorations and Applications Level 3

LESSON 109 PRACTICE

Name _____

Write in the missing numbers. Use fractions, whole numbers, and mixed numbers.

① 0, $\frac{1}{2}$, 1, ☐, 2, $2\frac{1}{2}$

② 3, $3\frac{1}{2}$, ☐, $4\frac{1}{2}$, ☐

③ 1, $1\frac{1}{3}$, $1\frac{2}{3}$, 2, ☐, ☐, ☐

④ 5, $5\frac{1}{3}$, ☐, ☐, ☐, $6\frac{2}{3}$

⑤ 2, ☐, $2\frac{1}{2}$, $2\frac{3}{4}$, ☐, $3\frac{1}{4}$, ☐, 4

⑥ 0, $\frac{1}{4}$, ☐, ☐, 1, ☐, $1\frac{3}{4}$, ☐

⑦ 0, ☐, $\frac{2}{5}$, ☐, $\frac{4}{5}$, ☐, $1\frac{1}{5}$

⑧ $6\frac{2}{5}$, ☐, ☐, ☐, $7\frac{2}{5}$, $7\frac{3}{5}$, ☐

What is the right sign? Draw <, >, or =.

⑨ $3\frac{1}{3}$ ◯ $3\frac{1}{2}$

⑩ $4\frac{1}{4}$ ◯ $3\frac{4}{5}$

⑪ $1\frac{1}{2}$ ◯ 2

⑫ $4\frac{1}{2}$ ◯ $4\frac{1}{2}$

⑬ $2\frac{1}{4}$ ◯ $2\frac{1}{2}$

⑭ $4\frac{3}{5}$ ◯ $5\frac{1}{4}$

⑮ $2\frac{1}{2}$ ◯ $3\frac{3}{4}$

⑯ $\frac{1}{2}$ ◯ $\frac{2}{5}$

LESSON 110 PRACTICE

Name _____

You may use manipulatives to solve these problems.

Max divided 16 marbles into 4 equal groups.

① How many marbles are there in each group? _____

② $\frac{1}{4}$ of 16 is _____

Then he divided 12 marbles into 4 equal groups.

③ Draw the 4 equal groups.

④ How many marbles are in each group? _____

⑤ $\frac{1}{4}$ of 12 is _____

⑥ $\frac{1}{3}$ of 15 is _____   ⑦ $\frac{1}{5}$ of 15 is _____

⑧ $\frac{1}{2}$ of 12 is _____   ⑨ $\frac{1}{3}$ of 12 is _____

⑩ $\frac{1}{2}$ of 8 is _____   ⑪ $\frac{1}{4}$ of 8 is _____

⑫ $\frac{1}{5}$ of 10 is _____   ⑬ $\frac{1}{2}$ of 10 is _____

⑭ $\frac{1}{2}$ of 16 is _____   ⑮ $\frac{1}{3}$ of 18 is _____

LESSON 111 PRACTICE

Name _____

What fraction is shaded?

1.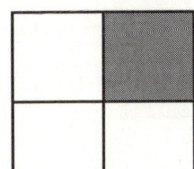

2.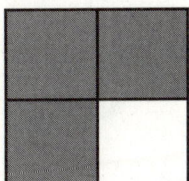

3.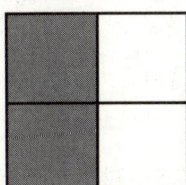

4.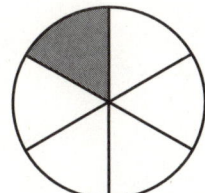

5.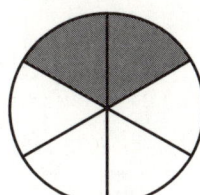

6.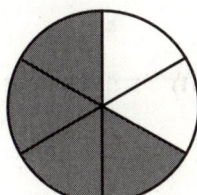

7.

8.

9.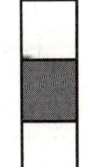

Math Explorations and Applications Level 3 • 111

LESSON 112 PRACTICE

Name _____

Solve.

1. $\frac{1}{3}$ of 15 = _____
2. $\frac{2}{3}$ of 15 = _____
3. $\frac{3}{3}$ of 15 = _____
4. $\frac{1}{4}$ of 16 = _____
5. $\frac{2}{4}$ of 16 = _____
6. $\frac{3}{4}$ of 16 = _____
7. $\frac{4}{4}$ of 16 = _____
8. $\frac{1}{4}$ of 40 = _____
9. $\frac{2}{4}$ of 40 = _____
10. $\frac{3}{4}$ of 40 = _____
11. $\frac{4}{4}$ of 40 = _____
12. $\frac{1}{2}$ of 6 = _____
13. $\frac{2}{2}$ of 6 = _____
14. $\frac{1}{5}$ of 10 = _____
15. $\frac{2}{5}$ of 10 = _____
16. $\frac{3}{5}$ of 10 = _____
17. $\frac{4}{5}$ of 10 = _____
18. $\frac{5}{5}$ of 10 = _____
19. $\frac{1}{2}$ of 14 = _____
20. $\frac{2}{2}$ of 14 = _____
21. $\frac{1}{2}$ of 18 = _____
22. $\frac{2}{2}$ of 18 = _____
23. $\frac{1}{4}$ of 8 = _____
24. $\frac{1}{2}$ of 8 = _____
25. $\frac{1}{6}$ of 12 = _____
26. $\frac{1}{3}$ of 12 = _____

112 • Math Explorations and Applications Level 3

LESSON 113 PRACTICE

Name _____

Solve. You may use manipulatives to help you.

1. $\frac{1}{3}$ of 12 = _____
2. $\frac{3}{10}$ of 40 = _____
3. $\frac{2}{4}$ of 8 = _____
4. $\frac{7}{10}$ of 40 = _____
5. $\frac{1}{2}$ of 16 = _____
6. $\frac{1}{2}$ of 10 = _____
7. $\frac{1}{6}$ of 24 = _____
8. $\frac{4}{5}$ of 50 = _____
9. $\frac{2}{6}$ of 24 = _____
10. $\frac{3}{3}$ of 18 = _____
11. $\frac{1}{8}$ of 24 = _____
12. $\frac{2}{4}$ of 36 = _____
13. $\frac{2}{8}$ of 24 = _____
14. $\frac{5}{5}$ of 45 = _____
15. $\frac{3}{8}$ of 24 = _____
16. $\frac{2}{5}$ of 25 = _____
17. $\frac{7}{8}$ of 24 = _____
18. $\frac{1}{6}$ of 12 = _____
19. $\frac{1}{5}$ of 35 = _____
20. $\frac{2}{3}$ of 12 = _____
21. $\frac{4}{5}$ of 35 = _____
22. $\frac{3}{4}$ of 12 = _____
23. $\frac{1}{10}$ of 40 = _____
24. $\frac{5}{6}$ of 12 = _____

Math Explorations and Applications Level 3

LESSON 114 PRACTICE

Name _____

What fraction is shaded?

1
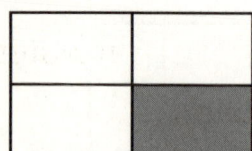

2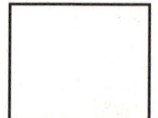
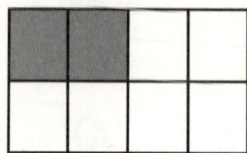

3
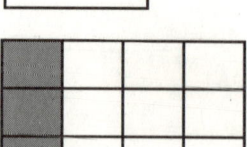

4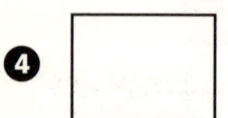
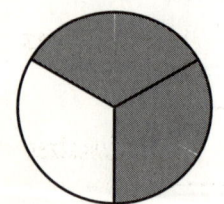

5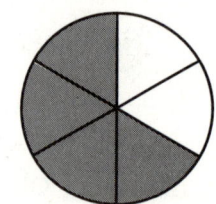

6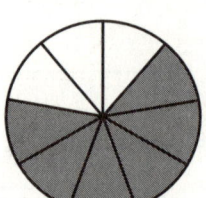

7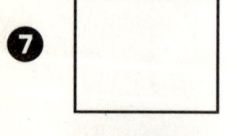
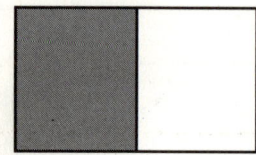

8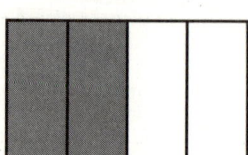

9

What is the right sign? Draw <, >, or =.

10 $\frac{1}{4} \bigcirc \frac{1}{3}$ **11** $\frac{1}{2} \bigcirc \frac{1}{3}$ **12** $\frac{1}{2} \bigcirc \frac{2}{4}$ **13** $\frac{1}{4} \bigcirc \frac{1}{6}$

14 $\frac{1}{10} \bigcirc \frac{1}{6}$ **15** $\frac{1}{2} \bigcirc \frac{2}{3}$ **16** $\frac{2}{6} \bigcirc \frac{1}{3}$ **17** $\frac{2}{4} \bigcirc \frac{3}{10}$

18 $\frac{4}{10} \bigcirc \frac{1}{2}$ **19** $\frac{3}{4} \bigcirc \frac{1}{6}$ **20** $\frac{3}{9} \bigcirc \frac{2}{3}$ **21** $\frac{1}{8} \bigcirc \frac{1}{4}$

PRACTICE Name _____

How many minutes?

① 1 hour = ☐ minutes   ② $\frac{1}{3}$ of an hour = ☐ minutes

③ $\frac{2}{3}$ of an hour = ☐ minutes   ④ $\frac{3}{3}$ of an hour = ☐ minutes

⑤ $\frac{1}{4}$ of an hour = ☐ minutes   ⑥ $\frac{2}{4}$ of an hour = ☐ minutes

⑦ $\frac{3}{4}$ of an hour = ☐ minutes   ⑧ $\frac{4}{4}$ of an hour = ☐ minutes

⑨ $\frac{1}{2}$ of an hour = ☐ minutes   ⑩ $\frac{1}{6}$ of an hour = ☐ minutes

Which is longer?

⑪ $\frac{1}{3}$ of an hour or $\frac{1}{2}$ of an hour? _____

⑫ $\frac{1}{2}$ of an hour or $\frac{1}{4}$ of an hour? _____

⑬ $\frac{2}{4}$ of an hour or $\frac{1}{2}$ of an hour? _____

⑭ $\frac{1}{5}$ of an hour or $\frac{1}{2}$ of an hour? _____

⑮ $\frac{3}{3}$ of an hour or $\frac{2}{3}$ of an hour? _____

LESSON 116 PRACTICE

Name _____

Solve. Watch the signs.

1. $7 \times 5 =$ _____
2. $15 - 7 =$ _____
3. $4 \times 9 =$ _____
4. $6 \times 0 =$ _____
5. $16 - 9 =$ _____
6. $16 + 9 =$ _____
7. $18 \div 9 =$ _____
8. $27 \div 3 =$ _____

What is the right sign? Draw <, >, or =.

9. 3.75 ◯ 37.5
10. 16.5 ◯ 1.6
11. 6.3 ◯ 6.30
12. 2.2 ◯ 3.0
13. 2.03 ◯ 3.02
14. 6.16 ◯ 616
15. 1.56 ◯ 1.05
16. 2.10 ◯ 2.1

Solve. Watch the signs.

17. 565 + 321
18. 8.36 + 7.26
19. 10.35 − 6.44

Solve.

20. 5 m = _____ cm
21. 437 cm = _____ m
22. 389 cm = _____ m
23. 2 m = _____ cm
24. $2.91 = _____ ¢
25. 312¢ = $ _____

LESSON 117 PRACTICE

Name _____

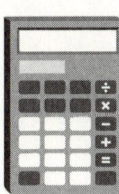

Add. Try to find a pattern. You may use your calculator.

① 1 + 3 + 5 + 7 + 9 + 11 + 13 + 15 + 17 + 19 + 21 = ☐

② 1 + 3 + 5 + . . . + 25 = ☐

③ 1 + 3 + 5 + . . . + 31 = ☐

④ 1 + 3 + 5 + . . . + 33 = ☐

⑤ 1 + 3 + 5 + . . . + 37 = ☐

⑥ 1 + 3 + 5 + . . . + 41 = ☐

⑦ 1 + 3 + 5 + . . . + 67 = ☐

⑧ 1 + 3 + 5 + . . . + 77 = ☐

⑨ 1 + 3 + 5 + . . . + 87 = ☐

⑩ 1 + 3 + 5 + . . . + 97 = ☐

Solve.

⑪ $\frac{1}{2}$ of 128 is ☐ ⑫ $\frac{1}{2}$ of 64 is ☐

⑬ $\frac{1}{2}$ of 32 is ☐ ⑭ $\frac{1}{2}$ of 16 is ☐

⑮ $\frac{1}{2}$ of 8 is ☐ ⑯ $\frac{1}{2}$ of 4 is ☐

LESSON 118 PRACTICE

Name _____

How many cubes? You may want to use cubes to build the figures.

❶ _____

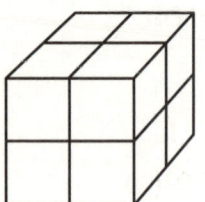

❷ _____

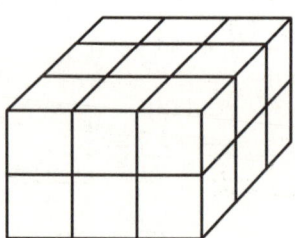

❸ _____

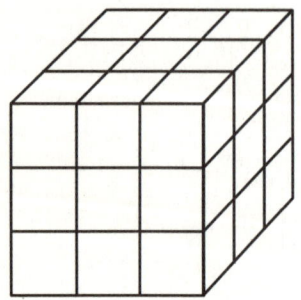

❹ _____

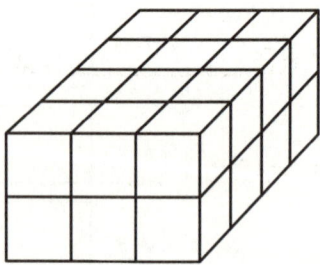

❺ _____

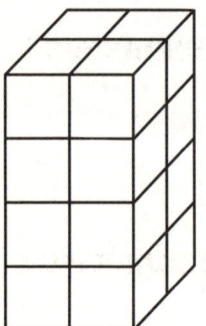

❻ _____

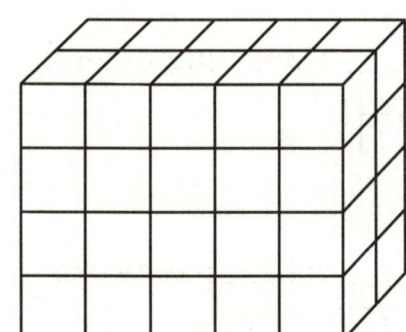

118 • *Math Explorations and Applications* Level 3

LESSON 119 PRACTICE

Name _____

The liter and milliliter are units of volume.
1000 mL = 1 L

Solve.

① 1 L = [ ] mL

② [ ] L = 2000 mL

③ [ ] L = 4000 mL

④ 5 L = [ ] mL

⑤ 8 L = [ ] mL

⑥ [ ] L = 6000 mL

Write the name of the unit that makes sense. Use cm, m, km, mL, L, or kg.

⑦ 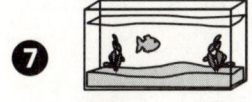 contains about 40 _____ of water.

⑧  is about 180 _____ tall.

⑨  weighs about 2 _____.

⑩  is about 15 _____ tall.

The cube has a volume of 1 cubic centimeter.

What is the volume of each box?

⑪ _____ cubic centimeters
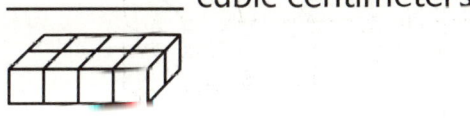

⑫ _____ cubic centimeters

⑬ _____ cubic centimeters
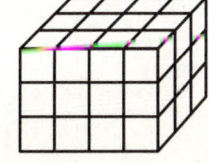

⑭ _____ cubic centimeters

LESSON 120 PRACTICE

Name _____

The cup, pint, quart, and gallon are units of volume.

There are 2 cups in 1 pint.

There are 2 pints in 1 quart.

There are 4 quarts in 1 gallon.

Solve.

① 2 pints = ☐ cups

② ☐ quarts = 8 cups

③ ☐ cups = 1 gallon

④ 6 pints = ☐ quarts

⑤ $\frac{1}{2}$ gallon = ☐ quarts

⑥ $\frac{1}{4}$ gallon = ☐ pints

⑦ ☐ pints = 5 quarts

⑧ 8 cups = ☐ pints

Draw a line from each unit of volume to a container on the table that can hold that much.

⑨ About 1 gallon

⑩ About 1 quart

⑪ About 1 cup

⑫ About 1 pint

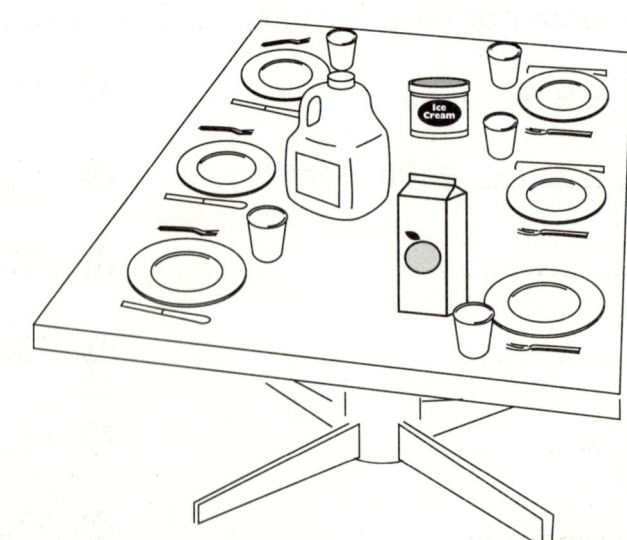

LESSON 121 PRACTICE

Name _____

Write the Arabic numeral for each of these Roman numerals.

I = 1   C = 100   V = 5   D = 500
X = 10   M = 1000   L = 50

❶ IV _____   ❷ XI _____   ❸ XXX _____

❹ XVI _____   ❺ XL _____   ❻ LXXI _____

❼ XXVIII _____   ❽ LXV _____   ❾ CCX _____

❿ CM _____   ⓫ MCCC _____   ⓬ DCV _____

⓭ CCCXL _____   ⓮ MDX _____   ⓯ CLVI _____

⓰ MLV _____   ⓱ MMMDC _____

⓲ MCMXC _____

Write the Roman numeral for each of these Arabic numerals.

⓳ 8 _____   ⓴ 23 _____

㉑ 42 _____   ㉒ 85 _____

㉓ 130 _____   ㉔ 721 _____

㉕ 553 _____   ㉖ 1320 _____

㉗ 2010 _____   ㉘ 60 _____

㉙ 900 _____   ㉚ 1700 _____

Math Explorations and Applications Level 3 • 121

LESSON 122 PRACTICE

Name _____

Solve. Watch the signs.

① 8 + 7 = _____
② 13 − 8 = _____
③ 14 − 7 = _____
④ 6 + 8 = _____
⑤ 12 − 3 = _____
⑥ 4 + 6 = _____
⑦ 3 + 8 = _____
⑧ 17 − 9 = _____
⑨ 7 + 2 = _____
⑩ 18 − 9 = _____
⑪ 5 + 6 = _____
⑫ 8 + 6 = _____

Multiply.

⑬ 8 × 7
⑭ 5 × 9
⑮ 3 × 7
⑯ 5 × 6
⑰ 2 × 8

⑱ 6 × 6
⑲ 4 × 3
⑳ 5 × 8
㉑ 9 × 4
㉒ 6 × 3

Divide.

㉓ 6)24
㉔ 8)40
㉕ 2)12
㉖ 5)45

㉗ 4)36
㉘ 3)18
㉙ 7)35
㉚ 9)36

LESSON 123 PRACTICE

Name _____

Solve. Watch the signs.

①   6243　　②   8917　　③   1300　　④   668
   − 913　　　　　+ 415　　　　　− 750　　　　　+ 812

⑤   7210　　⑥   7060　　⑦   1120　　⑧   900
   + 1083　　　　+ 8080　　　　− 1110　　　　− 400

⑨   470　　⑩   562　　⑪   40,000　　⑫   300
   + 30　　　　　+ 565　　　　− 39,990　　　− 199

⑬   75　　⑭   30　　⑮   125　　⑯   490
      75　　　　　　30　　　　　125　　　　　　10
      75　　　　　　30　　　　　125　　　　　490
   + 75　　　　　+ 30　　　　+ 125　　　　+ 10

LESSON 124 PRACTICE

Name _____

Solve these problems.

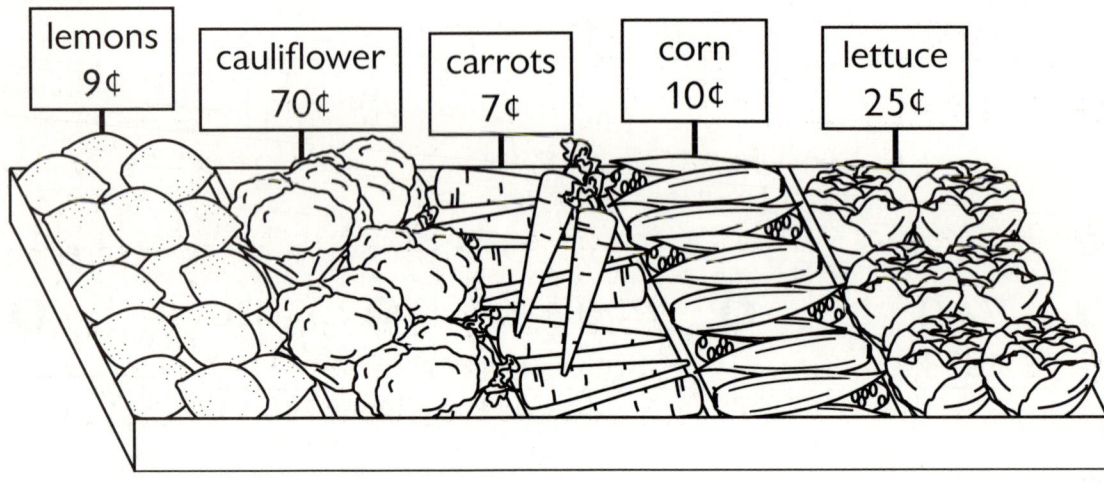

lemons 9¢ | cauliflower 70¢ | carrots 7¢ | corn 10¢ | lettuce 25¢

1 How much will four heads of lettuce cost? _____

2 How much will eight lemons cost? _____

3 How much will six carrots cost? _____

4 How much will three lemons and one cauliflower cost? _____

5 How much will five carrots and four ears of corn cost? _____

6 How much will two heads of lettuce, three carrots, and one lemon cost? _____

7 How much will one cauliflower, two ears of corn, and one carrot cost? _____

8 How much will seven carrots, one head of lettuce, and two lemons cost? _____

124 • Math Explorations and Applications Level 3

LESSON 125 PRACTICE

Name _____

Solve. Watch the signs.

1. $8 \times 7 =$ _____
2. $20 \div 5 =$ _____
3. $14 \div 7 =$ _____
4. $6 \times 8 =$ _____
5. $0 \times 3 =$ _____
6. $80 \div 10 =$ _____
7. $3 \times 8 =$ _____
8. $72 \div 9 =$ _____
9. $48 \div 6 =$ _____
10. $18 \div 9 =$ _____
11. $5 \times 6 =$ _____
12. $4 \times 3 =$ _____
13. $10 \times 5 =$ _____
14. $8 \div 1 =$ _____
15. $12 \div 3 =$ _____
16. $4 \times 6 =$ _____
17. $1 \times 7 =$ _____
18. $63 \div 9 =$ _____
19. $5 \times 9 =$ _____
20. $32 \div 8 =$ _____
21. $36 \div 4 =$ _____
22. $7 \times 7 =$ _____
23. $3 \times 8 =$ _____
24. $30 \div 6 =$ _____

Math Explorations and Applications Level 3

LESSON 126 PRACTICE

Name _____

The following map is a scale drawing of Big County. The driving routes between cities are shown.

Scale: $\frac{1}{4}$ inch = 20 miles

Solve these problems.

1. What is the distance between Allentown and Riverton? _____

2. What is the distance between Allentown and Maryville? _____

3. What is the distance between Edmonds and Grenville? _____

4. What is the distance between Highland and Danville? _____

5. What is the shortest route between Maryville and Petersville? _____

6. What is the distance between Highland and Riverton? _____

7. What is the distance between Collegetown and Orangetown? _____

8. What is the distance between Allentown and Grosspoint? _____

126 • Math Explorations and Applications Level 3

LESSON 127 PRACTICE

Name _____

1 Point to where these two lines will meet.

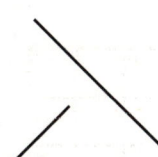

2 Where will these two lines meet?

3 Point to where these two lines will meet.

4 Where will these two lines meet?

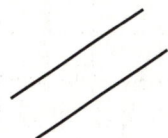

For each of the following figures count the number of line segments and the number of angles.

5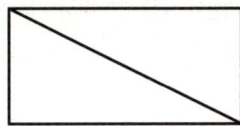

_____ line segments

_____ angles

6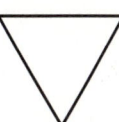

_____ line segments

_____ angles

7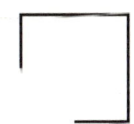

_____ line segments

_____ angles

8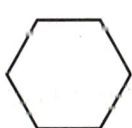

_____ line segments

_____ angles

Math Explorations and Applications Level 3

LESSON 128 PRACTICE

Name _____

Name the figures you find in each drawing. The figures will be squares, rectangles, parallelograms, trapezoids, and circles.

① 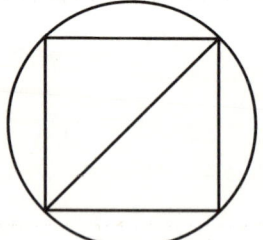 _____

② 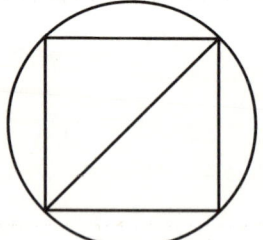 _____

③ 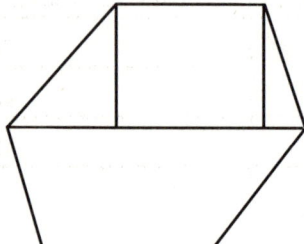 _____

④ 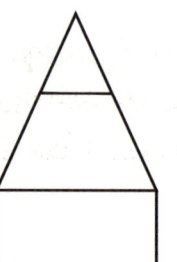 _____

LESSON 129 PRACTICE

Name _____

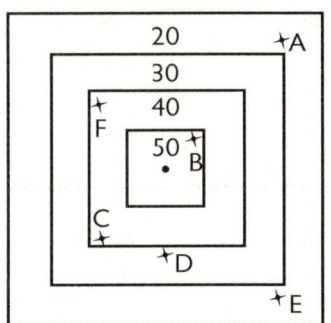

Reggie played a game of darts with Richard. They used this dartboard. Find the score for each dart. Use a centimeter ruler to measure the distance from each dart to the center.

Reggie		
Dart	Score	Distance from Center
A		mm
B		mm
C		mm
Total		

Richard		
Dart	Score	Distance from Center
D		mm
E		mm
F		mm
Total		

1 Who had the higher total score? _____

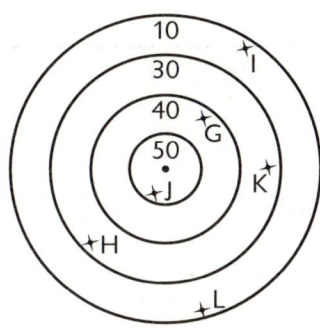

Jane played a game of darts with Tammy. They used this dartboard. Find the score for each dart. Measure the distance from each dart to the center.

Jane		
Dart	Score	Distance from Center
G		mm
H		mm
I		mm
Total		

Tammy		
Dart	Score	Distance from Center
J		mm
K		mm
L		mm
Total		

2 Who had the higher total score? _____

LESSON 130 PRACTICE

Name _____

Use a centimeter ruler to find the diameter and radius of each circle. Fill in the blanks and complete the chart.

1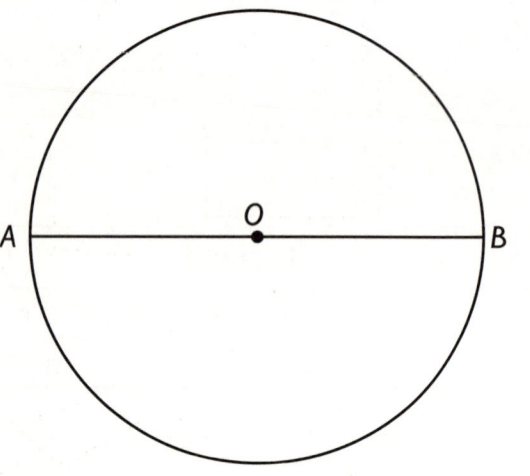

diameter: _____ radius: _____

4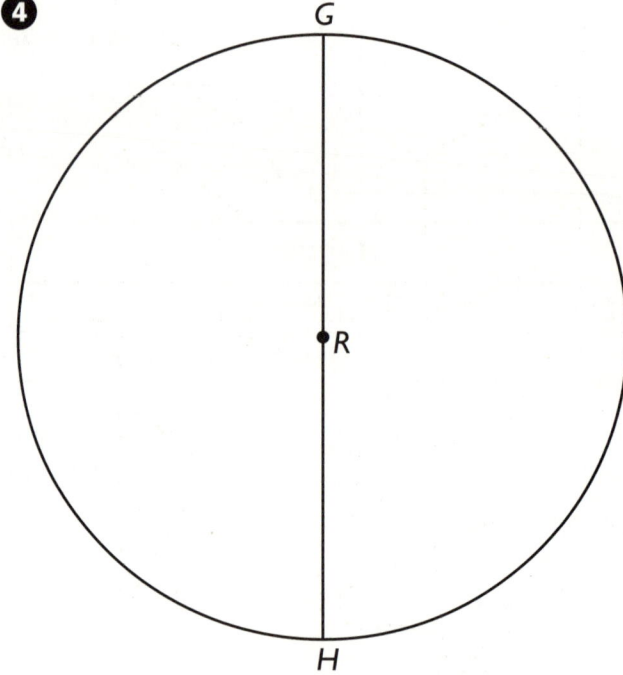

diameter: _____ radius: _____

2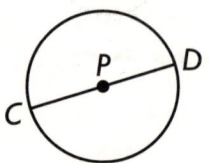

diameter: _____ radius: _____

Circle	Length of Diameter		Length of Radius	
1. O	AB =	cm	OB =	cm
2. P	CD =	cm	PD =	cm
3. Q	EF =	cm	QF =	cm
4. R	GH =	cm	RH =	cm

3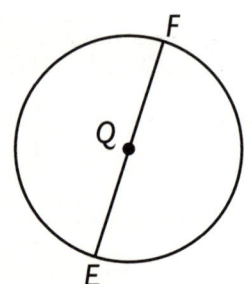

diameter: _____ radius: _____

5 What do you notice about the length of the diameters compared with the length of the radii?

_____
_____
_____

130 • Math Explorations and Applications Level 3

LESSON 131 PRACTICE

Name _____

Look at the figures below. Use tracing paper to help you see which figures are congruent. List each pair of congruent figures.

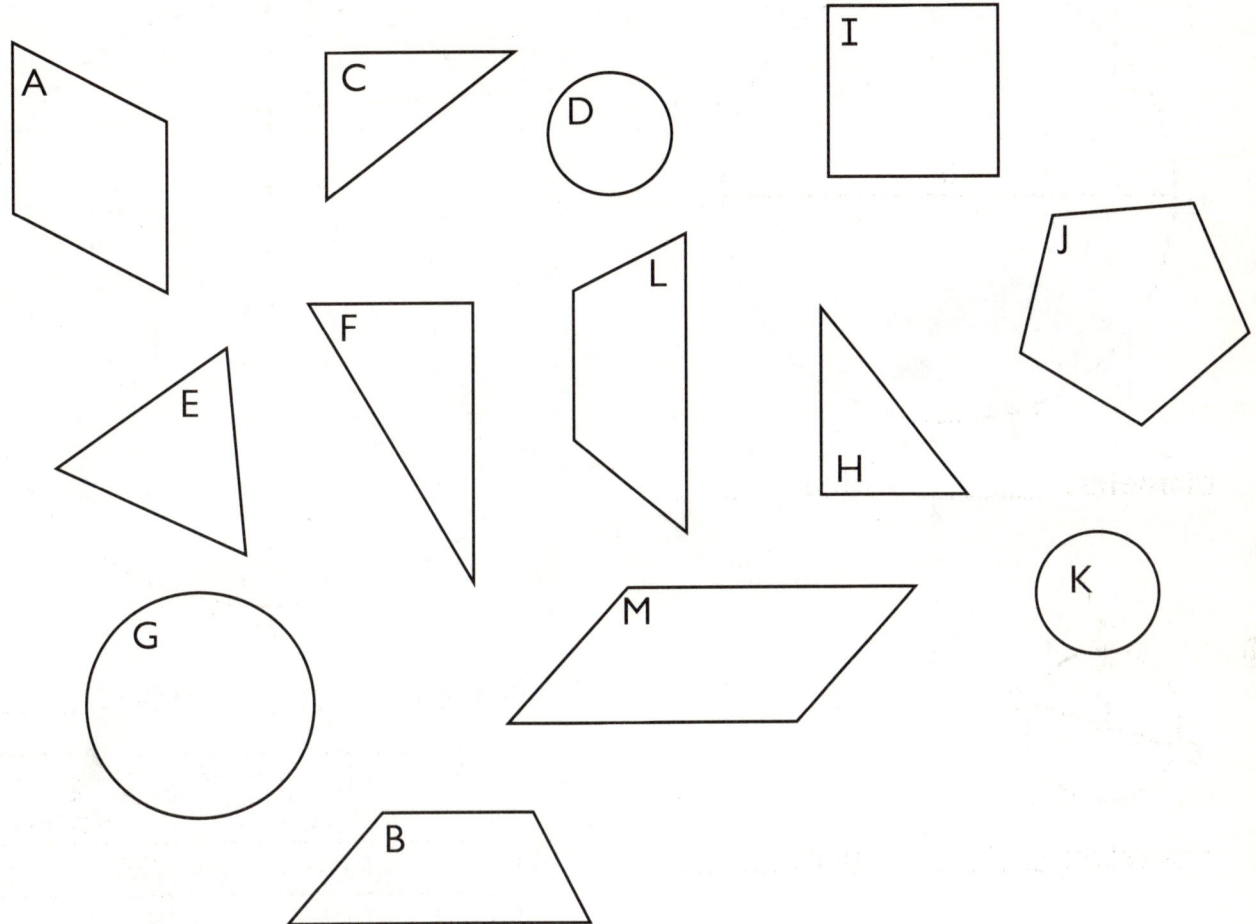

The congruent figures are _____.

LESSON 132 PRACTICE

Name _____

Draw all lines of symmetry in a color that is different from the drawing. Write the number of lines of symmetry.

1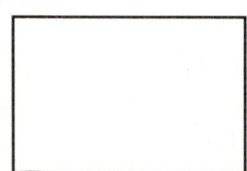

_____ line(s) of symmetry

2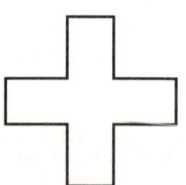

_____ line(s) of symmetry

3

_____ line(s) of symmetry

4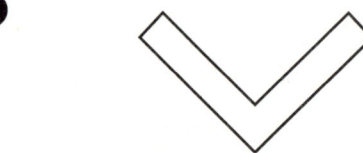

_____ line(s) of symmetry

5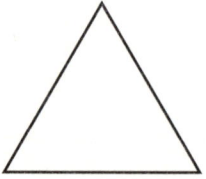

_____ line(s) of symmetry

6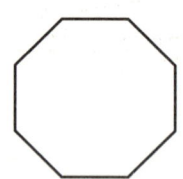

_____ line(s) of symmetry

7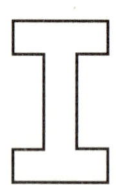

_____ line(s) of symmetry

8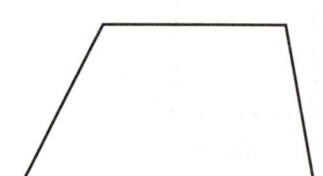

_____ line(s) of symmetry

9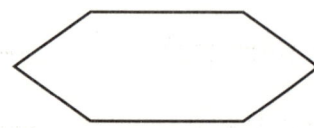

_____ line(s) of symmetry

10

_____ line(s) of symmetry

Math Explorations and Applications Level 3

LESSON 133 PRACTICE

Name _____

Answer the questions for each figure.

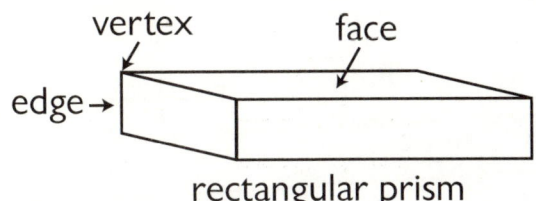
rectangular prism

1. How many vertices? _____
2. How many edges? _____
3. How many faces? _____

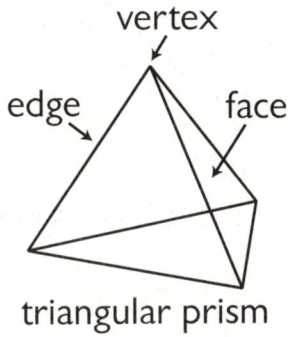
triangular prism

4. How many vertices? _____
5. How many edges? _____
6. How many faces? _____

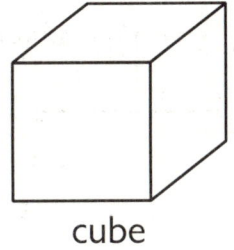
cube

7. How many vertices? _____
8. How many edges? _____
9. How many faces? _____

square pyramid

10. How many vertices? _____
11. How many edges? _____
12. How many faces? _____

Math Explorations and Applications Level 3 • **133**

LESSON 134 PRACTICE

Name _____

Find the area of each figure.

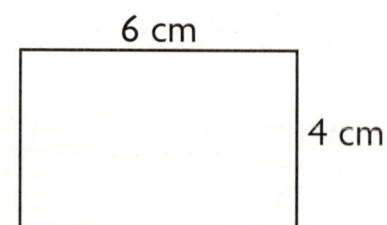

❶ ☐ square centimeters

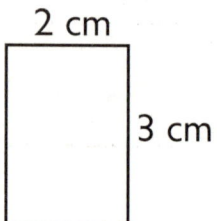

❷ ☐ square centimeters

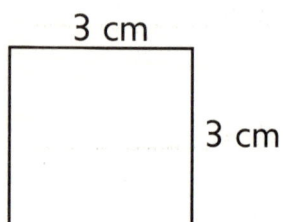

❸ ☐ square centimeters

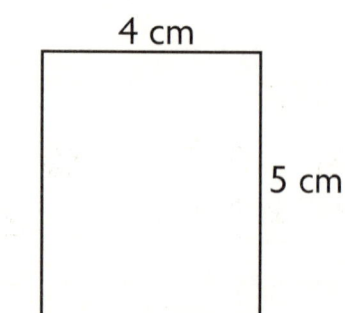

❹ ☐ square centimeters

Use the figure below to find each area.

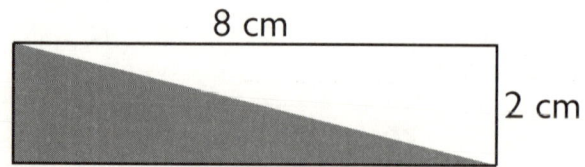

❺ Area of rectangle =
☐ square centimeters

❻ Area shaded =
☐ square centimeters

Use the figure below to find each area.

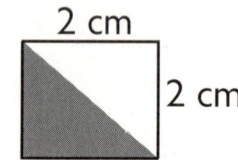

❼ Area of rectangle =
☐ square centimeters

❽ Area shaded =
☐ square centimeters

LESSON 135 PRACTICE

Name _____

Multiply.

① 9 × 4 = _____

② 10 × 3 = _____

③ 7 × 6 = _____

④ 4 × 8 = _____

⑤ 8 × 2 = _____

⑥ 9 × 6 = _____

⑦ 4 × 6 = _____

⑧ 8 × 9 = _____

⑨ 5 × 8 = _____

⑩ 3 × 3 = _____

⑪ 3 × 9 = _____

⑫ 7 × 4 = _____

⑬ 6 × 8 = _____

⑭ 0 × 5 = _____

⑮ 10 × 6 = _____

⑯ 6 × 6 = _____

⑰ 3 × 1

⑱ 7 × 9

⑲ 8 × 3

⑳ 4 × 4

㉑ 7 × 8

㉒ 2 × 7

㉓ 4 × 3

㉔ 5 × 6

㉕ 8 × 8

㉖ 6 × 2

Math Explorations and Applications Level 3 • **135**

LESSON 136 PRACTICE

Name _____

Multiply. You may draw pictures to help. Discuss whether your answers are reasonable.

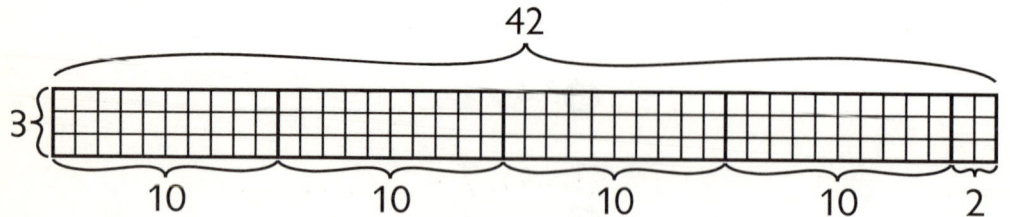

❶ 42
  × 3

❷ 50   **❸** 35   **❹** 32   **❺** 40   **❻** 22
 × 7   × 9   × 7   × 6   × 8

❼ 61   **❽** 44   **❾** 51   **❿** 90   **⓫** 16
 × 6   × 3   × 8   × 4   × 3

⓬ 86   **⓭** 34   **⓮** 23   **⓯** 15   **⓰** 72
 × 1   × 4   × 2   × 5   × 2

136 • Math Explorations and Applications Level 3

LESSON 137 PRACTICE

Name _____

Solve. Watch the signs.

1) $9 \times 7 =$ _____

2) $63 \div 7 =$ _____

3) $28 \div 7 =$ _____

4) $4 \times 7 =$ _____

5) $6 \times 3 =$ _____

6) $18 \div 3 =$ _____

7) $7 \times 5 =$ _____

8) $35 \div 5 =$ _____

9) $48 \div 6 =$ _____

10) $8 \times 6 =$ _____

11) 7
    + 8

12) 6
    + 5

13) 12
    − 4

14) 9
    − 3

15) 17
    − 9

16) 34
    × 6

17) 27
    × 3

18) 52
    × 2

19) 16
    × 5

20) 70
    × 9

LESSON 138 PRACTICE

Name _____

Solve these problems.

① Farmer Brown has 18 cows. Each cow has four legs. How many legs are there all together on Farmer Brown's cows? _____

② Jenny received $45 from her grandmother, $45 from her parents, and $45 from her cousins for her birthday. How much money did Jenny receive? _____

③ Scott has 24 $5 bills. Does he have enough money to buy the bike? _____

④ Mrs. Johnson baked 6 dozen muffins. How many muffins did she bake all together? _____

⑤ Admission to the science museum is $4. How much will it cost for 29 students to go to the museum? _____

⑥ A plane can seat six people in a row. There are 35 rows. How many people can the plane seat? _____

Math Explorations and Applications Level 3

LESSON 139 PRACTICE

Name _____

Multiply. Use shortcuts when possible. Compare and discuss your methods. Which are easiest?

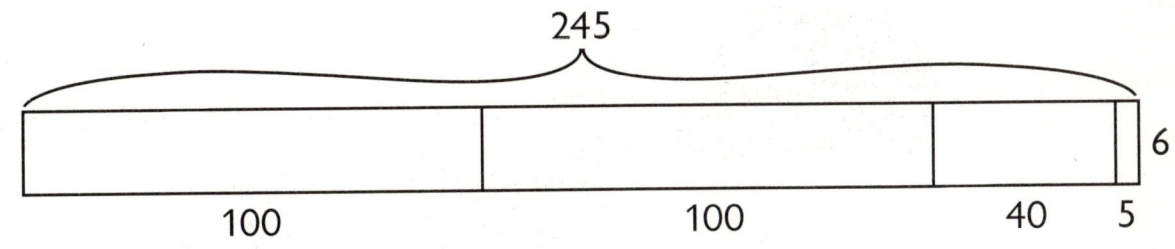

$$600 + 600 + 240 + 30$$

1) 245
× 6

2) 354
× 3

3) 205
× 9

4) 213
× 7

5) 438
× 2

6) 512
× 4

7) 701
× 6

8) 834
× 0

9) 125
× 8

10) 260
× 4

11) 136
× 3

12) 586
× 1

13) 721
× 4

14) 150
× 6

15) 903
× 4

16) 679
× 2

LESSON 140 PRACTICE

Name _____

Multiply. Use shortcuts when possible.

① 75
× 8

② 62
× 9

③ 350
×   4

④ 210
×   7

⑤ 89
× 5

⑥ 538
×   1

⑦ 97
× 6

⑧ 408
×   3

⑨ 246
×   2

⑩ 50
× 9

⑪ 74
× 3

⑫ 301
×   5

Solve these problems.

⑬ There are 426 flowers in the field. Each flower has eight petals. How many petals are there all together? _____

⑭ There are five levels in a parking garage. Each level holds 223 cars. How many cars can the parking garage hold? _____

140 • Math Explorations and Applications Level 3

LESSON 141 PRACTICE   Name _____

 **Solve these problems.**

❶ Mr. Morris earns $685 each week. How much does he earn in six weeks? _____

Most years have 365 days. Leap years have 366 days. Leap years come every four years.

❷ Maggie is exactly nine years old. How many days old is Maggie? _____

❸ If Shanna eats three meals of 750 calories each, how many calories will Shanna eat? _____

❹ If 1 kilogram of pears costs 198 cents, how many cents would it cost to buy 4 kilograms of pears? _____

❺ Amy can swim 100 yards in 128 seconds. How long would it take her to swim 500 yards? _____

❻ Ginger eats about 135 grams of cat food each day. About how many grams does Ginger eat in a week? _____

Math Explorations and Applications Level 3 • **141**

LESSON 142 PRACTICE

Name _____

Multiply.

① 95
  × 4

② 32
  × 9

③ 54
  × 3

④ 27
  × 5

⑤ 80
  × 2

⑥ 49
  × 7

⑦ 31
  × 8

⑧ 29
  × 6

⑨ 422
  × 6

⑩ 765
  × 2

⑪ 320
  × 8

⑫ 704
  × 7

⑬ 282
  × 3

⑭ 238
  × 5

⑮ 157
  × 4

⑯ 417
  × 9

 **Solve these problems.**

⑰ If Becky saves $2 a day for one year, how much will she save? _____

⑱ If Becky saves $2 a day for four years, how much will she save? _____

142 • Math Explorations and Applications Level 3

LESSON 143 PRACTICE

Name _____

 You know that for all numbers, *n* and *m*, $n + m = m + n$. Here are some examples. Solve.

① $8 + 6 =$ _____   ② $6 + 8 =$ _____

③ $20 + 18 =$ _____   ④ $18 + 20 =$ _____

⑤ $745 + 389 =$ _____ ⑥ $389 + 745 =$ _____

⑦ Does $n - m = m - n$? _____

You know that for all numbers, *n* and *m*, $n \times m = m \times n$. Here are some examples. Solve.

⑧ $5 \times 4 =$ _____   ⑨ $4 \times 5 =$ _____

⑩ $10 \times 8 =$ _____   ⑪ $8 \times 10 =$ _____

⑫ $112 \times 435 =$ _____   ⑬ $435 \times 112 =$ _____

⑭ Does $n \div m = m \div n$? _____

 Solve. You may use your calculator.

⑮ $2^6 =$ _____   ⑯ $6^2 =$ _____

⑰ $3^4 =$ _____   ⑱ $4^3 =$ _____

⑲ $8^3 =$ _____   ⑳ Is it true that for all numbers *n* and *m*, $n^m = m^n$? _____

LESSON 144 PRACTICE

Name _____

Multiply. You may draw pictures to help. Discuss whether your answers are reasonable.

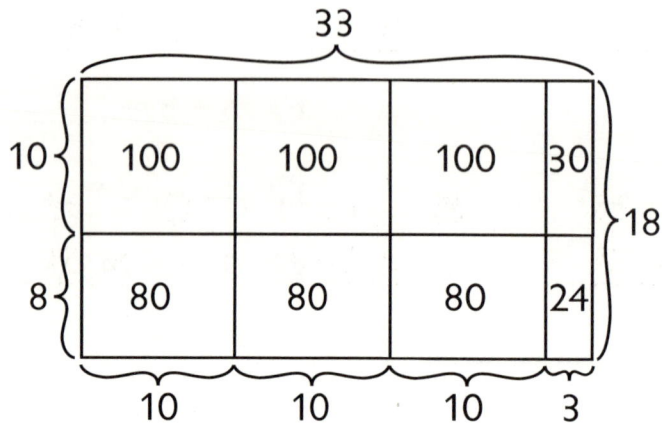

1) 33
× 18

2) 42
× 27

3) 35
× 19

4) 32
× 71

5) 45
× 45

6) 22
× 63

7) 81
× 14

8) 22
× 44

9) 15
× 15

10) 42
× 23

11) 16
× 33

12) 86
× 11

13) 34
× 24

14) 92
× 51

15) 37
× 68

16) 42
× 59

144 • Math Explorations and Applications Level 3

LESSON 145 PRACTICE

Name _____

Multiply.

1. 7
   × 8

2. 6
   × 5

3. 9
   × 4

4. 3
   × 8

5. 2
   × 7

6. 40
   × 23

7. 35
   × 14

8. 65
   × 20

9. 33
   × 51

10. 11
    × 61

Solve. Watch the signs.

11. 8999
    + 8999

12. 1265
    + 4935

13. 4076
    − 1889

14. 835
    − 788

15. 681
    + 493

16. 2000
    + 2000

17. 8004
    − 3552

18. 3230
    − 2230

Solve these problems.

19. Lai has $1354 in her savings account. Paul has $967 in his savings account. How much more money does Lai have? _____

20. Mike collects aluminum cans for recycling. He has three bags of 366 cans. How many cans has Mike collected? _____

Math Explorations and Applications Level 3 • 145

LESSON 146 PRACTICE

Name _____

Solve these problems.

① George wants to buy 12 packs of gum. Each pack costs 35¢. How much will the gum cost all together? _____

② Write that amount in dollars and cents. _____

③ There are 36 inches in 1 yard. How many inches are there in 18 yards? _____

④ A 2-pound box of spaghetti serves 11 people. How many people would 15 boxes of spaghetti serve? _____

⑤ A box contains 32 pens. How many pens would 14 boxes contain? _____

⑥ Willis has 13 quarters. How many dollars and cents is that worth? _____

There are 16 ounces in 1 pound.

⑦ Maria weighs 54 pounds. How many ounces does Maria weigh? _____

⑧ Maria's dog weighs 38 pounds. How many ounces does Maria's dog weigh? _____

LESSON 147 PRACTICE

Name _____

Multiply.

1) 2.47 × 8

2) 1.64 × 5

3) 1.35 × 4

4) 3.09 × 6

5) 2.36 × 3

6) 7.6 × 3

7) 3.5 × 4

8) 6.2 × 8

9) 3.1 × 5

10) 1.9 × 6

11) 9.00 × 2

12) 5.5 × 6

13) 1.25 × 9

14) 2.11 × 7

15) 6.3 × 5

 **Solve these problems.**

16) One box of cereal costs $3.19. How much do six boxes cost? _____

17) One sandwich costs $2.49. How much do four sandwiches cost? _____

18) One computer desk is 1.82 meters long. How many meters long are five desks placed end to end? _____

LESSON 148 PRACTICE

Name _____

What is the right sign? Draw <, >, or =.

1. 6×1.45 ◯ 6×2
2. 17×18 ◯ 16×16
3. 3.5×3.5 ◯ 3×3
4. 4.67×9 ◯ 5×9
5. 65×23 ◯ 65×13
6. 81×72 ◯ 8.1×7
7. 1.21×4 ◯ 121×4
8. 20×20 ◯ 100×4
9. 7.95×0 ◯ 8×0
10. 0.65×2 ◯ 6.50×2
11. 29×30 ◯ 29×3
12. 87×22 ◯ 80×20
13. 1.06×10 ◯ 2×10
14. 4.3×6 ◯ 3.4×6
15. 163×5 ◯ 163×4
16. 31×15 ◯ 13×15
17. 42×71 ◯ 71×42
18. 2.01×3 ◯ 201×3
19. 5×8 ◯ 5.50×8
20. 42×35 ◯ 34×42

 **Solve these problems.**

Jackie has $5.00 to buy vegetables for a party snack tray. Carrots cost $1.09 per bunch. Cucumbers cost $1.49 each. Green peppers cost 53¢ each.

21. Can she buy one bunch of carrots, one cucumber, and three green peppers? _____

22. If she was only buying carrots, how many bunches could she buy? _____

LESSON 149 PRACTICE

Name _____

In each problem two of the answers are clearly wrong and one is correct. Choose the correct answer.

1 6245 + 3400 = _____
   a. 9045   b. 9645   c. 10,175

2 6031 − 1200 = _____
   a. 4000   b. 4831   c. 5009

3 74.3 + 14.9 = _____
   a. 8.92   b. 892   c. 89.2

4 12 − 1.5 = _____
   a. 10.5   b. 6.25   c. 4.5

5 40 × 8 = _____
   a. 32   b. 320   c. 48

6 352 × 4 = _____
   a. 1200   b. 1208   c. 1408

7 63 × 21 = _____
   a. 1230   b. 1323   c. 1503

8 26 × 70 = _____
   a. 1820   b. 2820   c. 1280

Solve these problems.

9 Mrs. Zoran has a $20 bill. A bottle of juice costs $2.79. Does she have enough money to buy eight bottles of juice? _____

10 The math club wants to raise $200 by selling popcorn. Will the club raise enough money if it sells 75 boxes of popcorn at $2.25 each? _____

Math Explorations and Applications Level 3 • **149**

Count up. Fill in the missing numbers.

1. | 98 | 99 | 100 | 101 | 102 | 103 | 104 |

2. | 998 | 999 | 1000 | 1001 | 1002 | 1003 |

3. | 9998 | 9999 | 10,000 | 10,001 | 10,002 | 10,003 |

4. | 10,997 | 10,998 | 10,999 | 11,000 | 11,001 | 11,002 |

5. | 899,998 | 899,999 | 900,000 | 900,001 | 900,002 |

6. | 909,999 | 910,000 | 910,001 | 910,002 | 910,003 |

7. | 999,997 | 999,998 | 999,999 | 1,000,000 | 1,000,001 |

8. | 1,099,998 | 1,099,999 | 1,100,000 | 1,100,001 | 1,100,002 |

LESSON 151 PRACTICE

Name _____

Complete the chart.

	Amount (in dollars)	Amount (in cents)
1	5	
2	500	
3	5000	
4	25	
5	250,000	

Add.

6   67
    + 95

7   89
    + 41

8   18
    + 75

9   6
    + 8

10   12
    + 9

11   644
    + 108

12   345
    + 815

13   290
    + 567

14   138
    + 747

15   1570
    + 2330

16   2462
    + 1640

17   56,421
    + 39,990

18   23,652
    + 45,248

19   428,347
    + 686,714

20   789,523
    + 654,829

21   5,120,345
    + 4,965,006

22   45,819,432
    + 17,304,005

23   6,263,170
    + 2,133,551

24   59,709,528
    + 22,616,039

25   6,004,256
    + 7,090,628

LESSON 152 PRACTICE

Name _____

Subtract.

❶ 85
  − 27

❷ 16
  − 9

❸ 98
  − 75

❹ 24
  − 8

❺ 123
  − 96

❻ 814
  − 438

❼ 513
  − 327

❽ 724
  − 560

❾ 96,430
  − 74,710

❿ 8700
  − 2800

⓫ 23,875
  − 12,925

⓬ 6,435,187
  − 4,203,752

Use the table below to answer each question.

Counties of New York City	Population
Bronx	1,203,789
Brooklyn	2,300,664
Manhattan	1,487,536
Queens	1,951,598
Staten Island	378,977
Total	7,322,564

⓭ What is the difference in the populations of Queens and the Bronx? _____

⓮ What is the difference in the populations of Manhattan and Staten Island? _____

⓯ What is the difference in the populations of New York City and Brooklyn? _____

LESSON 153 PRACTICE

Name _____

Multiply.

① 9   ② 7   ③ 8   ④ 9   ⑤ 7
× 8   × 6   × 4   × 5   × 8

Divide.

⑥ 8)56   ⑦ 7)14   ⑧ 4)32   ⑨ 3)18   ⑩ 9)81

⑪ 63 ÷ 9 = _____   ⑫ 54 ÷ 6 = _____

⑬ 20 ÷ 2 = _____   ⑭ 48 ÷ 8 = _____

Solve. Watch the signs.

⑮   1145   ⑯   283,427   ⑰   5288
   + 7721   − 66,578   − 4320

⑱   6725   ⑲   9,981,057   ⑳   7,215,711,457
   − 3886   + 2,288,488   + 5,314,788,396

Math Explorations and Applications Level 3 • 153

LESSON 154 PRACTICE

Name _____

Use this code to answer the following riddle.

A	B	C	D	E	F	G	H	I	J	K	L	M
21	14	42	25	9	17	26	10	56	18	3	11	19
N	O	P	Q	R	S	T	U	V	W	X	Y	Z
4	7	16	15	8	24	6	22	13	2	12	20	5

Teacher: Why did you bring your math homework to exercise class?
Student:

__ __ __ __ __ __ __ __ __ __ __ __ __
1   11 14 7 18   2 12   3 17 19 13 5 9

__ __ __ __   __ __ __ __ __ __ __ __ __ .
21 24 15 6   10 20 23 4 16 25 8 22 26

① $7 \times 8 =$ _____   ② $18 \div 3 =$ _____
③ $83 - 75 =$ _____   ④ $6 \times 7 =$ _____
⑤ $21 \times 2 =$ _____   ⑥ $63 \div 7 =$ _____
⑦ $8 + 5 =$ _____   ⑧ $21 - 14 =$ _____
⑨ $18 \div 2 =$ _____   ⑩ $9 + 8 =$ _____
⑪ $5 \times 2 =$ _____   ⑫ $28 \div 4 =$ _____
⑬ $13 + 9 =$ _____   ⑭ $7 \times 3 =$ _____
⑮ $10 + 9 =$ _____   ⑯ $25 - 19 =$ _____
⑰ $3 \times 3 =$ _____   ⑱ $90 \div 10 =$ _____
⑲ $16 + 9 =$ _____   ⑳ $42 - 34 =$ _____
㉑ $4 \times 6 =$ _____   ㉒ $36 \div 9 =$ _____
㉓ $13 + 8 =$ _____   ㉔ $14 - 7 =$ _____
㉕ $18 + 38 =$ _____   ㉖ $12 \times 2 =$ _____

154 • Math Explorations and Applications Level 3